College and Career Readiness

College and Career Readiness

A Guide for School Counselors K–12

Cheryl Moore-Thomas

ROWMAN & LITTLEFIELD
Lanham • Boulder • New York • London

Published by Rowman & Littlefield
An imprint of The Rowman & Littlefield Publishing Group, Inc.
4501 Forbes Boulevard, Suite 200, Lanham, Maryland 20706
www.rowman.com

6 Tinworth Street, London SE11 5AL, United Kingdom

Copyright © 2019 by Cheryl Moore-Thomas

All rights reserved. No part of this book may be reproduced in any form or by any electronic or mechanical means, including information storage and retrieval systems, without written permission from the publisher, except by a reviewer who may quote passages in a review.

British Library Cataloguing in Publication Information Available

Library of Congress Cataloging-in-Publication Data Available

ISBN: 978-1-4758-3291-4 (cloth) ISBN: 978-1-4758-3292-1 (pbk.) ISBN: 978-1-4758-3293-8 (electronic)

To all the school counselors I've met and those I've yet to meet who tirelessly work to make a positive difference in the lives of students; and to Steven Thomas, my loving husband, coach, cheerleader, and best friend.
You are my rock, Steve.

Contents

Preface	ix
PART I: COLLEGE AND CAREER READINESS: THEORY AND PRACTICE	**1**
1 Career and College Readiness Counseling in a Developmental Context	3
2 Access and Equity	7
3 Career Theory and Exploration	23
4 Building a Solid Foundation with School-Family-Community Partnerships	35
PART II: LESSONS, ACTIVITIES, AND APPROACHES FOR CAREER AND COLLEGE READINESS SCHOOL COUNSELING	**45**
5 College and Career Readiness in Elementary School	47
6 Individual Learning Plans	63
7 College and Career Readiness in Middle School	65
8 College and Career Readiness in High School	89
9 What Is Next?	113

Appendix: College and Career Planning Calendar	119
References	127
Index	133
About the Author	135

Preface

Why this book? Why now?

In January 2015, President Obama introduced an extraordinary yet compelling plan. He proposed a community college program that would make community college free for everyone who is willing to work for it. The president went on to say that we, as a nation, have a responsibility to make sure that everybody has the opportunity to train themselves for better jobs, better wages, and better benefits.

President Obama suggested that America's past success was in part built on the valuing and normalization of K–12 schooling, yet in today's complex society, K–12 education in and of itself is no longer sufficient. As a united people, we must have the educational preparation to continue to lead the world and tackle the issues and questions we face as a global society.

Continuing this conversation, the 2016 presidential campaign also proposed the need for affordable, accessible college education as a central theme of many of the candidates' platforms. Today, President Trump and key members of his administration are committed to engaging communities, colleges, universities, and businesses to partner in new, innovative ways that increase students' pathways to fulfilling and meaningful careers.

What excites me about these developments and new conversations about postsecondary opportunities for all students is that they underscore what we as counselors have known all along, what we held in our hearts as we entered fields dedicated to the positive growth and development of students. We know today, and we have always known, that we have no throwaway students. None are expendable. All are valuable. All can contribute. All deserve the opportunity to maximize their potential and reach their personal college and career goals.

Education is still one of the best keys to personal maximization. In today's world, education beyond the foundational preparation of K–12 schooling often is a bridge that leads learners from working poor conditions to greater economic security. On a global level, education leads to a greater level of national and global security and provides our learners with tools needed to face the economic, environmental, societal, and ethical challenges ahead.

Education changes lives, opens doors, and unleashes possibilities. It increases opportunities and lifestyle options. It opens minds to new ways of thinking and gives voice to new theories, inventions, and approaches that could literally one day save the world.

And while most would agree that education is a profound tool in the minds and hands of a skilled learner, we also know that we could do better at increasing the number of students who enroll in college and other postsecondary educational opportunities. We could do better at increasing students' awareness and preparation for rich career options. Systemic legacies of racism and bias, academic opportunity gaps, and economic and information barriers often prevent significant numbers of students from even considering college, postsecondary training opportunities, and rich career paths as realistic options for their own futures.

Why this book? Why now? I have written this book because we all know we can do better. We can and must do more to get students prepared for and enrolled in college and postsecondary educational opportunities. And we must create new pathways to success that meet the needs of our increasingly diverse student community.

As counselors, we possess the social capital and skill sets that can be used to positively effect change in the lives of our students. With our continued commitment and increasing skill set we can help each student open the door to a successful future. With skills and commitment, we can broaden the pool of students preparing for and entering college and careers from the academic elite and high fliers to everyone who is willing to work for it.

Laura Rendon, renowned scholar and thought leader on college access, noted, "By the time students get to 12th grade, it is too late to improve college-eligibility. It could be said that students begin to drop out of college in grade school" (1998, p. 61).

Together, we can help our students change that phenomenon. Through this book I outline the contributions school counselors and others make to the development and college and career readiness of each student at the elementary, middle, and high school levels.

College and career readiness is not the job of one subset of school counselors. It is critical that all school-based counselors work with students early and often to establish and reinforce college and career expectations and provide them with the experiences and supports they need to view college and career as attainable goals. This is work for all of us and this book shows one of the paths forward.

Part I

COLLEGE AND CAREER READINESS: THEORY AND PRACTICE

Chapter One

Career and College Readiness Counseling in a Developmental Context

This chapter situates college and career readiness counseling as a relevant and crucial work area for school counselors in kindergarten through high school settings. Debunking the notion that college and career readiness counseling begins in high school and is only possible and necessary for certain student populations, this chapter sets the stage for a developmental approach to college and career work with all K–12 students, including those from student populations that have been traditionally underrepresented and historically marginalized.

DEVELOPMENTAL CONTEXT

While current economic indicators appear to be on the uptick, our nation faces serious challenges regarding long-term economic growth and individual and family level economic security. Previously, it was not unusual for many individuals to enjoy long-term employment with a single organization or within a single career field.

Today, members of Generation Z, those born between 1995 and 2010, and Gen Alpha, those born after 2010, do not have the same job security outlook. While much has yet to be studied and written about these groups, it seems to be clear that members of these communities will compete in global markets. They will hold many different jobs over the course of their careers. They will perhaps be more entrepreneurial than previous generations. They will be more culturally diverse in terms of race, ethnicity, gender identity, sexual orientation, and religiosity than previous generations. And their paths to the world of work may be less traditional than has been seen in recent American history.

While these variables are likely to fluctuate for future generations, what is likely not to fluctuate is the national enduring, cultural valuing of a productive, satisfying career that allows each person to contribute in meaningful ways to personal development, family, local community, and nation. As students graduate from high school, they must have the knowledge, skills, and dispositions necessary to immediately and successfully enter the workforce, college, or other educational postsecondary experience (Arnold, Lu, & Armstrong, 2012). The world of today and tomorrow demands the active participation of all citizens. As a nation and a global society, the United States cannot afford to have any youth sit out or be cast aside.

In a very real sense, this demands that every student succeed. Cultural identities, geography, and socioeconomic circumstances of life can no longer determine which students have full access to effective college and career readiness pathways and which do not. As demographics in America change and as economic gaps between the haves and the have nots widen, the necessity of having all students well positioned for postsecondary life is imperative. Continued national productivity and vitality demand it.

Traditional models of school counseling positioned the work of preparing students for college and career readiness as largely the responsibility of high school counselors. Career fairs, college days, interest inventories, college testing information sessions, and resume writing lessons were activities built into school counseling programs almost exclusively at the high school level. Many in the field, however, have recognized that beginning this work at the high school level is far too late.

It would be relatively easy to simply begin the work of college and career readiness with younger students in middle or elementary school. But what if college and career readiness were not simply a series of activities offered to students in high school or middle and elementary school for that matter? What if college and career counseling were approached from a developmental perspective?

Many school counselors are familiar with developmental approaches. Most school counseling preparation programs have courses devoted to understanding and considering counseling implications for developmental models of human growth. These models consider a lifespan approach for human growth that embraces change, discovery, and an unfolding of deepening levels of awareness and purpose. Typically, developmental models include conceptual understandings of a series of stages, statuses, or phases of growth that move in a linear or spiraling progression. Each stage or status tends to involve key acts, stances, or challenges that are worked through or resolved before movement to the next stage or status. Each stage or status is characterized by different needs. Developmental models also typically rest on grounding principles that expressly value humanity and leave room for the integrity of individual paths.

Embedded in counselors' understandings of developmental models and the progression of students' growth is the understanding that psychosocial or emotional factors can delay or arrest development. Issues like trauma, illness, violence, poverty, and educational inequities can have profound effects on students' development related to academic achievement and college and career readiness. These topics and implications are beyond the scope of this book but must be considered by school counselors working to meet students' needs at all instructional levels.

Using the framework of developmental models, school counselors are also positioned to understand the importance of the counselor traits of authenticity, trust, respect, and clarity of purpose and expectation when working with students and families. Further, school counselors' familiarity with developmental approaches also means that they have a keen understanding of the role of context in development. Contextual matters of culture, identity, socioeconomics, geography, disposition, and ability among others are important to consider when thinking about development across a lifespan and student and counselor interactions.

Understanding developmental approaches creates an opportunity for school counselors and others committed to career and college readiness to reimagine the work in this area as a developmental process. This book offers a developmental approach to college and career readiness that embraces the very same principles of developmental theory regarding human growth: an across the lifespan approach, a commitment to an unfolding and changing discovery of self, a deep respect for humanity and individual paths, and a recognition of the importance of context and cultural identities.

The thread of developmental college and career readiness offers a bright future for students and the school counselors that are privileged to work with them. This work begins in the next chapter with a focus on cultural identities, access, and equity as foundations of developmental college and career counseling.

Chapter Two

Access and Equity

This chapter explores historical and current issues regarding access and equity in higher education for traditionally underrepresented populations including first generation college students, students with special needs, students of color, LGBTQ students, English language learners, and undocumented students. The chapter emphasizes advocacy and asset-based counseling approaches to the issues of access, equity, and diversity relevant to the work of school counselors and school-based college counselors for college and career counseling.

ACCESS AND EQUITY

Approximately 12 million of today's American college-going students enter college immediately upon graduation from high school. These traditional college students have often spent four years in one of our nation's high schools learning and setting the educational foundation for a lifetime of success. These students have seemingly met the expectations set by schools across the country; they have graduated college and are career ready. But is this true for all of our students?

College and career ready is a phrase often tossed around educators' conversations and school mission statements. College and career readiness implies that graduating students have the skills and dispositions necessary to immediately enroll and succeed in postsecondary courses or certificate programs that lead to career paths with opportunities for advancement and growth (Arnold, Lu, & Armstrong, 2012).

College and career readiness is an important, complex issue. It poses many opportunities for school counselors and others involved with college and career counseling to partner with teachers, families, administrators, and other stakeholders to help students meet readiness goals. It is within this context that the issues of *access* and *equity* regarding college and career opportunities for students become of paramount importance.

K–12 enrollment data show that while across our nation many students have attended high schools steeped in the tradition and historical legacies of their communities, the students themselves are very different from the students of a generation ago. Today's students come from a K–12 public school population that is more diverse than ever. The 2014 public school population was majority non-White, a first in our nation's history. This demographic trend is expected to continue.

Also important to note are recent findings from the Program for International Student Assessment (PISA). These data from measurements of 15-year-old students around the world in mathematics, science, and reading literacy show students' abilities to apply their learning and solve real-world problems. The 2015 test administration found that the average U.S. score in reading was lower than the average in 14 other countries. In science the U.S student average was lower than that of 18 other countries. In mathematics, the U.S. student average was lower than that of students in 36 other countries (NCES, PISA 2015 Results).

These academic achievement data are critical for school counselors to understand as school counselors often play a key role in gate keeping, course selection, course registration, and helping students access courses and curriculum (e.g., algebra, calculus, advanced science courses, honors programs) that increase opportunity rather than limit it. Knowledge of these important academic achievement trends will also help school counselors better help students make connections between academic proficiencies and skills that will enhance students' ability to achieve and ultimately result in students' college and career readiness and the ability to compete in a global career market.

While current and future students hold the key to continued greatness in the American story, they also provide school counselors and educators with exciting opportunities to face the new age of school-based college and career counseling with approaches and interventions that meet the needs of a diverse student body.

This chapter explores historical and current issues regarding access and equity in higher education for historically underrepresented traditionally aged student populations. The chapter then continues with a discussion of advocacy and asset-based counseling approaches to the issues of access, equity, and diversity relevant to the work of school counselors and others in the area of college and career counseling.

WHAT IS ACCESS AND EQUITY IN HIGHER EDUCATION?

Access and equity in higher education is the opportunity for admission and success for historically underrepresented student populations that is fair and just given the opportunity for access and success for all other students in higher education. Access and equity speaks to the fairness and inclusiveness in opportunity that exists independent of race, ethnicity, socioeconomic status, gender, sexual identity, religious affiliation, or other factors. Beliefs in access and equity in education broadly, and higher education more specifically, are hallmarks of the American life and signatures of success attainment.

Recent trends in higher education seem to suggest, however, that as a nation America may no longer be moving toward goals of accessible and equitable collegiate opportunities for all deserving students. In fact, American higher education is more socioeconomically stratified today than at any time during the past three decades (Austin & Oseguera, 2004). Moreover, charges of reverse discrimination and the dismantling of affirmative action policies along with mounting college costs and dwindling financial aid resources have chipped away at the college enrollments of students of color and students from other underrepresented communities (Allen, 2005).

In some cases, only the lucky or financially well off have been able to go to college. This phenomenon has yielded a current college landscape where the college student population is majority White, even though the K–12 public school population is majority non-White (U.S. Department of Education, NCES, 2013). These startling statistics represent an inequity in our educational system that is detrimental.

Inequality in higher education affects economic and social well-being as well as global security. If America is to maintain its position as a global leader, all of its students must be able to contribute fully to the knowledge economy through maximal educational opportunities that include college and career paths. In order to maintain a nation that is productive and thriving economically, socially, and culturally, all Americans, including those from diverse backgrounds, must have access to and opportunities for rich postsecondary experiences and career security.

Who, then, are America's students? The following section provides a brief overview of the rich, diverse backgrounds from which many of today's students come.

First Generation College Students

First generation college students, students whose parents have not completed a college degree, are a significant population in American colleges and universities. Recent data show first generation college students when compared to their non–first generation college peers are more likely to be, but are not exclusively, Black or Hispanic (Chen, 2005). It is important, therefore, to make no assumptions about who is a first generation college student. Today's diverse first generation students are about 34% of the college freshman class, up approximately 12 percentage points from the number of first generation college students in the freshman class of 2000 (Lightweis, 2014; Blackwell & Pinder, 2014).

While this is good news, in many cases first generation college students face significant challenges to college attendance. Perhaps most significant of these are parental expectations and lack of experience regarding college attendance.

Since their parents did not attend college, first generation college students cannot benefit from their parents' first-hand college application and navigation experiences. Their parents cannot share personal stories of challenge and success in college to help guide and inform their children's goal setting and behaviors for accessing college. Additionally, for a host of reasons including but not limited to parental expectations and educational backgrounds, first generation students may have financial obligations, job responsibilities, academic remediation needs, lower high school achievement test and college entrance exam scores, and social readiness concerns that further challenge their college access.

First generation college students may also be less likely than their peers to seek or receive support and basic guidance from a school counselor on common college admission practices or connections between career goals and educational requirements. School counselors and others committed to college and career access, however, can support first generation college students in meaningful ways.

School counselors and other college and career counseling professionals can recognize the specific student needs of first generation college students and address them with sensitivity, skill, and evidence-based practices that provide students and families with practical information, and also provide them with the high expectations and encouragement that make college and career goals accessible. Many of these practices are discussed later in this chapter.

Students with Low Income

The Department of Health and Human Services issues annual guidelines for poverty based on family size and geographic area. These guidelines vary slightly from year to year, but current low-income guidelines for families of four start at around $47,000. According to recent census data, about half of all Americans are at or below low-income levels with a disproportionate percentage of these being Americans of color.

While the college and career plans for students with low income hold great promise for their economic stability and the collective global economy, students with low family incomes also face a number of challenges beyond fewer economic resources than their peers. Data suggest that students of low-income backgrounds are often less prepared academically than students of more advantaged economic backgrounds, highlighting a disconnect between the common rhetoric of academic rigor and "college and career readiness for all," and the reality of the academic experience of many low-income students (Berg, 2010).

Funding practices used in many regions to allot money to schools and determine per student spending rates are based on property taxes and, by extension, the economic wealth in an area. These funding practices in part explain the lack of honors and advanced placement classes, the relatively low numbers of highly qualified teachers, the nonexistence of arts and music programs, and the very limited availability of school-based student and family support services, including counselors, in many schools serving students with low family income.

Together, these factors and practices work to sustain the disconnect between educational rhetoric and students' lived experiences regarding the articulated educational commitment to college and career readiness for all students.

Students Experiencing Homelessness

Rates of homelessness have increased nationally. Recent estimates suggest that as many as 2.5 million children experience homelessness every year (National Center on Family Homelessness, 2014). School counselors are well aware of some of the challenges students and families experiencing homelessness navigate when facing school. Proof of residency, immunization and health records, consistent attendance, and reliable transportation are but a few of the challenges that make enrolling and succeeding in school difficult. Unfortunately, many students experiencing homelessness also face depression, anxiety, and feelings of loss and disconnection from their friends and communities (Havlik, Schultheis, Schneider, & Neason, 2016).

The McKinney-Vento Homeless Assistance Act, passed in 1987 and reauthorized in 2015, provides guidance and support for students experiencing homelessness. Under the act students have the right to receive free, appropriate education; to enroll in school immediately even if they do not have the documents normally required for school admission; to receive transportation to and from school; and to receive educational support services according to their needs.

Importantly, the act also requires that high school students experiencing homelessness receive college readiness information and counseling; and information about financial aid, the college application process, and college campus supports. School counselors would be well served to become familiar with and advocate for the various aspects and resources associated with McKinney-Vento given the importance of this kind of preparation in the context of a comprehensive, developmental college and career readiness program.

Students with Special Learning Needs

The National Center for Education Statistics reports that approximately 13% of children and adolescents receive disability support services in public schools (U.S. Department of Education, 2015). Looking more deeply into these data, we find that about 6% of public school students are diagnosed with a learning disability or attention deficit disorder (2015). Perhaps due to better identification processes and early intervention, these two diagnoses have risen significantly over the past thirty years, almost doubling to current rates and representing the largest group of students with special needs receiving services in public schools today.

The *DSM-5* defines a learning disorder as persistent difficulties in reading, writing, arithmetic, or mathematical reasoning skills during formal years of schooling that are not explained by developmental, neurological, sensory (vision or hearing), or motor disorders. These difficulties significantly interfere with academic achievement, occupational performance, or activities of daily living.

Students with learning disabilities may demonstrate inaccurate or slow, labored reading; poor written expression; difficulties remembering number facts; or inaccurate mathematical reasoning (see "Specific Learning Disorder" fact sheet, American Psychiatric Association, 2013). About two-thirds of all students with identified learning disorders are male.

Students with attention deficit disorder or attention deficit hyperactivity disorder demonstrate difficulty staying focused, controlling behavior, and reducing hyperactivity. Attention deficit disorder (ADD) and attention deficit/hyperactivity disorder (ADHD) are brain-based disorders. It is estimated that as many as one-third of those with learning disabilities also have ADHD. Boys are more likely than girls to be diagnosed with either ADD or ADHD.

Students with other special learning needs are seen in smaller numbers in today's public schools. Specifically, students with speech and language needs make up about 3% of the public school population. Students with hearing, visual, and orthopedic needs make up about 0.3% of the population, collectively. Students with mental retardation make up about 1% of the public school population, representing a slight decline in identified students of late (U.S. Department of Education, NCES, 2015). Autism, a diagnosis that has been recognized more frequently in students in the K–12 public school population in recent years, is on the rise, moving to about 0.9% of the population (2015).

Students with special learning needs may face tremendous challenges, but it is important to note that many students with special learning needs can have very rewarding and successful careers in college and the world of work. School counselors must be ever mindful that appropriate diagnosis and accommodation helps students have the opportunity to meet their potential for college and career readiness.

Assessment, diagnosis, intervention, and accommodation, when provided in culturally relevant ways, begins to appropriately level the playing field for students with special learning needs. Through child study teams and other interdisciplinary support processes, educational professionals, school counselors, and college and career specialists in K–12 schools must work to ensure that happens.

Students of Color

Students of color now comprise a larger percentage of public school students than White students. Out of approximately 50 million public school students in 2014, about 50.3% are African American, Hispanic, Asian/Pacific Islander, Native American, Native Alaskan, and multiracial. While changes in the racial/ethnic geographic distribution of public school enrollment does differ, generally Hispanic and Asian/Pacific Islander student enrollment is increasing in all geographic regions (Northeast, Midwest, South, and West) and Black student enrollment is fluctuating slightly or decreasing in all regions (U.S. Department of Education, NCES, 2013).

Given these trends, it is expected that the number of high school graduates will follow a pattern similar to the public school enrollment patterns. Currently, however, these K–12 public school demographic trends do not seem to be translating to college enrollment trends. This pattern may strongly indicate continuing inequities (Wang, 2014). This may be especially true for particular segments of the students of color population including Black and American Indian/Alaska students who have alarmingly low high school graduation rates and college completion rates.

Continuing inequities challenge school counselors and educators to help change this disturbing trend and increase college and career readiness and college enrollment for all students of color. The "What Should Counselors

Do?" section of this chapter suggests specific ways school counselors and school-based college counselors can begin this important work and support students of color toward goals of college and career readiness and access.

LGBTQ Students

Lesbian, gay, bisexual, transgender, and questioning (LGBTQ) students greatly contribute to the diversity of today's American schools. Research practices including challenges with identity labeling make it difficult to accurately assess the number of LGBTQ students in K–12 schools. Reasonable estimates of the population range from 3% to 10% of students in K–12 public schools (Cianciotto & Cahill, 2003; Sanlo & Espinoza, 2012).

As is true for all student populations, the LGBTQ student population is diverse and individual students' experiences vary based on personal demographics and community factors. What is unfortunately true for many, however, is that school environments remain a distressing place. On a recent survey regarding school climate, over 55% of LGBT students reported feeling unsafe because of their sexual orientation; and nearly 65% reported hearing homophobic remarks often or frequently (Kosciw, Greytak, Palmer & Boesen, 2014).

Threats, harassment, and discriminatory behavior along with noninclusive and marginalizing school policies may cause LGBTQ students to avoid school activities, become truant, experience depression or anxiety, and fail to maximize their academic potential and mental health well-being. Research strongly suggests that LGBTQ students who feel safe and affirmed in school perform better in school (Kosciw, Greytak, Palmer & Boesen, 2014). Counselors and others focused on college and career readiness for children and adolescents have a key role and responsibility in this work. Specific practices are discussed in a following section.

Immigrant Students

First and second generation immigrant students are about 19% of the K–12 public school student population (U.S. Department of Education, NCES, 2011). First generation students and their parents were born in a country other than the United States. Second generation students were born in the United States, but their parents were born elsewhere. Together, the first and second generation immigrant student population in the United States, often identified as "immigrant students" in the research literature, has increased and has contributed significantly to public school population growth in recent years.

Immigrant families often come to the United States seeking the American dream of improved educational and economic opportunities. Recent immigrants have come from a number of regions including East Asia, South Central Asia, Western Europe, Canada, Australia, Mexico, Central America, the Dominican Republic, Haiti and other parts of the Caribbean, Middle East, and Africa.

Backed with a strong work ethic and diverse educational histories (about 29% of immigrant fathers and 26% of immigrant mothers have earned a college degree in their native country while approximately 31% of immigrant mothers have not graduated from high school), immigrant families plant roots across the United States with many families locating in the western United States (Hernandez & Napierala, 2012). Some may have connections with and the help of family and cultural community members already well established in the United States. Others face the challenges of finding a home, employment, schools, and ways of understanding American culture all on their own. Unfortunately, limited economic resources and limited English often make these important tasks even more difficult.

To address a piece of this challenge, many immigrant students, about four million or 9% according to recent estimates, participate in school-based programs for English language learners (ELL) (U.S. Department of Education, NCES, 2014). While immigrant students with English language learning needs attend public schools throughout the nation's cities, suburbs, and rural areas, the states with recent high growth in population of immigrant students receiving English language services include Nevada, South Carolina, Delaware, Arkansas, North Carolina, Alabama, Mississippi, and Virginia (Horsford & Sampson, 2013).

ELL services are clearly crucial, not just in the nation's high growth areas, but across the country. Along with these services must come a respect of diverse cultures and a high level of cultural competence that permeates the language instruction. This level of cultural competence is important in K–12 approaches to college and career counseling.

Undocumented Students

Undocumented students are those who have entered the United States without legal documentation. Often undocumented students have been brought or sent to the United States by their families in search of increased economic and educational opportunities. While it is difficult to estimate the number of undocumented students in America, data suggest that over 65,000 undocumented students graduate from high school each year with only about 5% to 10% of the population immediately entering college (Barnhardt, Ramos & Reyes, 2013; Nguyen & Serna, 2014). Currently, about 75% of all undocumented students come from Latin American countries.

In 1982 the Supreme Court ruled that undocumented children and young adults have the same right to attend public primary and secondary schools as do U.S. citizens. As a result of this groundbreaking case, *Plyler vs. Doe,* undocumented students may not be denied admission or access to enrollment in public elementary and secondary schools, may not be required to disclose or document their immigration status, must not be charged tuition or a fee based on citizenship status, and must not be required to show or disclose a social security number.

While undocumented students have open access to public elementary and secondary schools, they may not have such access to college. Today, only California, Illinois, Kansas, Nebraska, New Mexico, New York, Oklahoma, Texas, Utah, Washington, and Wisconsin offer in-state tuition rates for undocumented students. Three of these states, New Mexico, Oklahoma, and Texas, go further by providing state financial assistance to undocumented students. Without this support, undocumented students who are college bound are faced with international student tuition rates, which often are many times greater than tuition rates for U.S. citizens and legal residents.

These tuition costs are often prohibitive for undocumented students and their families. Moreover, deepening the financial burden, federal regulation does not permit undocumented students to receive federal financial assistance of any kind for college.

Many undocumented students and their families have contributed greatly to their communities and the local economy. Studies suggest that undocumented students attain levels of achievement, leadership, and civic engagement that equal or exceed that of their peers (Perez, 2010). Anecdotal records show many undocumented students demonstrate daily, admirable measures of personal resilience, academic determination, and optimism about future successful college and career journeys.

In order to be able to continue to strengthen their economic and civic contributions and meet these dreams for future success, undocumented students must have reasonable access to higher education and careers that pay a living wage.

WHAT SHOULD COUNSELORS DO?

School counselors and school-based college counselors have a special role in ensuring access and equity for the diverse student populations discussed above. This work is critical as it may be one of just a few resources or forms of *social capital* students can spend in their pursuit of postsecondary options.

Social Capital

Social capital refers to the resources that flow through relationship ties. These ties can be through personal relationships like those students have with counselors or teachers, or ties through organizations or networks. Important information like how to select classes that lead to desired career goals, or how to select an appropriate college and fill out the college application, or how to dress and discuss personal strengths at a job interview often flow through these ties to enhance students' functioning and success. In general, social capital ties lead to important information, norms, and support.

Families are generally the primary source of social capital for students. School, however, is also important in the lives of K–12 students. School counselors and school-based college counselors are perfectly positioned to serve as significant resources of social capital related to college and career readiness for all students, including the specific student populations discussed in this chapter (Bryan, Moore-Thomas, Day-Vines, & Holcomb-McCoy, 2011; Croninger & Lee, 2001).

Counselor guidance, advocacy, and support specifically related to career and college readiness can provide the strong network and social capital that supplements family networks when students' families have limited information or resources. The underlying key to school counselors as a rich and meaningful source of social capital for students is the counselor–student relationship.

Counseling Relationship

As school counselor caseloads have increased and job expectations have broadened, school counselors may not have the time to make the personal connections with students that serve as the very essence of strong counseling programs and the foundation of important social capital opportunities. It is essential that school counselors at all levels *make* the time to connect with students and form the kind of effective professional school counseling relationships that encourage students to explore and pursue their career interests and goals. Over an entire K–12 experience, this kind of encouraged and facilitated developmentally appropriate exploration can lead to students who do in fact graduate college and are career ready.

In the age of high stakes testing and very large counselor caseloads, this is often easier said than done. However, counselors must use the skills they gained during their educational programs to create, plan, and advocate for comprehensive school counseling programs that are mission centered, data driven, and importantly, student focused.

This demands that students—not reports, disciplinary roles, or administrative responsibilities—remain central. Student-centered college and career readiness interventions and programs like individual and small group counseling sessions on decision making, classroom guidance lessons on college and career choice, special programs for college visits, mentors or community business partnerships, and student internships allow time and opportunity for school counselors to make genuine, personalized connections that are key to students and their healthy development in ways that paperwork completion and monitoring duties and patrols are not.

School counselors and college counselors who know their students well and open doors to meaningful self-learning experiences and community-based opportunities for student engagement and exploration have an increased opportunity to meet students where they are developmentally. School counselors who work in this fashion also open doors to students' postsecondary access.

Advocacy

The inefficient and costly practice of using counselors' time and unique skill set in non-counseling-related tasks (i.e., lunch room monitoring, test material organization, bus duty) reduces the amount of time that school counselors can spend in college and career counseling, and consequently reduces college and career readiness and access for students. School counselors and school-based college counselors must clearly see themselves as contributors to the academic mission of their schools. They must work with school administrators to advocate for changes in counselors' roles that support direct counseling services to students and increase counselor time for student-centered college and career readiness interventions and programs.

Counselors' advocacy extends beyond role clarification. School counselor advocates have important work to do regarding access and equity. In pursuit of serving as an advocate, multicultural counseling theory and practice offers counselors specific insight and approaches for appropriate, culturally relevant school-based counseling. Multicultural counseling approaches recognize the role of culture in the lives of students and operate from a perspective that honors that positionality. Counselor self-awareness coupled with racial and cultural identity development theory, evidenced-based practices, and culturally competent skills, enable counselors to respond to the student populations described in this chapter in effective ways.

One of the most effective ways to advocate for students of color, LGBTQ students, immigrant students, students with special learning needs, and others from historically marginalized student populations is to serve as an advocate who is diligent and committed to address and eradicate prejudice, bias, discrimination, and oppression as it manifests in the schoolhouse and lives of students.

At the elementary level this could mean running diverse school counseling groups that allow students to develop prosocial behaviors within their unique cultural context. Or it could involve making sure families receive clear and thorough information regarding their child's specific needs and plans for learning. At the secondary level this could mean leading classroom guidance and individual counseling sessions that help students examine their beliefs and goals with an understanding and affirmation of who they are as cultural beings.

Across all levels of instruction, true advocacy demands the monitoring of school policies and practices (i.e., course placement, disciplinary action, retention) to ensure that they are free from bias and discrimination, and that there is facilitation of a school environment that is strong and supportive enough to allow students to openly discuss their experiences and feelings related to discrimination, intolerance, and bias. Specifically, school counselors and school-based college counselors can spearhead teams that analyze schoolwide data on disciplinary actions, drop-out rates, and grade retentions to make sure that unintended bias regarding students does not manifest in school policies and practices.

Of course, school behavior policies and practices, advanced and honors classes placement practices, as well as extracurricular and enrichment opportunities must be free from overt and covert bias, discrimination, and oppression. However, before these issues can be approached in an authentic manner, students and families must be welcomed into the conversation and the review of these school-based policies and practices so that their voices and experiences are recognized, heard, valued, and considered. This means counselors must be ever ready and prepared to take a lead role in facilitating uncomfortable yet significant conversations about race, gender bias, oppression, or intolerance among students, families, colleagues, and other school personnel.

In particular, school harassment and bullying data seem to suggest that counselors should increase efforts to broach these difficult conversations in advocacy of LGBTQ students. School counselors and others can help LGBTQ students meet college and career readiness goals by partnering with their school-based colleagues and community leaders to think about and challenge school policies and practices that marginalize gender nonconforming students such as those related to dress code, dances, and bathroom use (Payne & Smith, 2012), and make certain all students have access to inclusive school curriculum that affirms the identities, histories, and legacies of all people.

Moreover, to work effectively in this area, school counselors must ensure that their own counseling practice is inclusive and responsive to the needs of LGBTQ students. This requires advocacy, but it also requires a continued commitment to counselor professional development in the area of multicultural counseling through coursework, conference training and workshops, advanced reading, and clinical supervision.

Once the foundation of strong, culturally competent student–counselor relationships with all students has been established, school counselors and school-based college counselors can move forward the goals of access and equity as determined by the needs of their particular student population. Prior to the development of this foundation, access and equity goals run the risk of emerging simply as "to-dos" or annual programs that do not effectively meet the needs or touch the lives of diverse students.

Far too many career and college access outreach programs and special initiatives fail because they do not center on the relationship ties and issues of advocacy that are necessary for authentic work in school communities.

In Context Experiences

Exposure to rich and diverse options is a privilege that students from underrepresented or historically marginalized communities often do not enjoy at the same rate as their peers. At the elementary school level this could mean working with classroom teachers to extend curriculum-based cultural activities and field trips in social studies or science to pre- and postactivity discussions of related careers or educational paths that recognize and address the developmental needs of students.

As an example of this kind of developmentally appropriate opportunity, imagine that fourth grade students while preparing for their field trip to the state historical museum are also guided to think about the work of the docent that leads their tour. The students could prepare questions not only about the museum content, but also about the job of a docent or other museum professionals. This informal class interview could be followed by writing a journal entry on what it might be like to work in a museum.

This kind of activity moves the traditional elementary school career exploration to an "in context" experience that allows young students to gain exposure to careers while making meaningful connections to their daily lives and activities. For students of underrepresented communities in particular, this extension and maximization of extracurricular learning is critical as it makes the most of experiences that are often far too rare in the lives of students.

Information

In addition to in context experiences, school counselors and school-based college counselors must provide accurate, relevant information regarding college access and career readiness. Many times, counselors mistakenly believe all students have access to information that in some communities is commonly known or understood regarding college and careers.

For example, members of some of the student populations discussed in this chapter may benefit from counselor created workshops and newsletters provided in multilingual versions that review accurate and updated information about college costs and financial aid possibilities, including information on existing private and nongovernmental funding sources for college and career scholarships, awards, and paid apprenticeships and other training opportunities.

Parent and guardian nights or workshops explaining fees and timelines for common college application processes or career entrance exams may also help meet the needs of students and their families. Additionally, evening or weekend "office hours" with counselor and technology availability to help students and families complete required forms and applications for college and postsecondary careers may help students and families get the one-on-one assistance and information that will help open a pathway to a successful career or college journey.

Transition Planning

Traditionally, school-based counselors may think of transition planning as a mandatory multistakeholder process exclusively for high school students with special learning needs. In this traditional context, transition planning helps students with special learning needs lay out a path toward a successful postsecondary college or career experience.

Transition planning, however, is a best practice for all students and in particular the students discussed in this chapter. Counselors must help students consider their course selections, college and career goals, interests, resumes, entrance exam requirements, and other elements that help lead them toward postsecondary life.

Individual learning plans (ILPs) are tools counselors can use to help students in this process. ILPs, briefly discussed later in this book, hold particular promise for the students discussed in this chapter because they give school counselors, college counselors, students, and families opportunities to closely examine the strengths and needs of a student in ways that provide maximized access and equity opportunities through a thoughtfully considered and carefully monitored college and career counseling process.

Skills

Students' inter- and intrapersonal skill development falls squarely in the domain of school counselors' work. Through individual counseling, small group counseling, and classroom guidance, school counselors have the unique opportunity to help students develop key skills and levels of awareness that are essential for career and college access.

Goal setting skills, study skills, self-monitoring skills, social skills, and time management skills can be approached through individual and group counseling. Decision making and career exploration curricula fit appropriately into school counseling guidance programs in K–12 settings. Moreover, students can explore interests, motivation, resiliency, and culturally competent coping strategies in individual counseling sessions that may introduce planning for postsecondary opportunities. It is through this specialized work that school counselors have the unique opportunity and responsibility to offer the kind of motivating personalized encouragement and setting of high expectations that help catapult all students toward satisfying opportunities in college and career.

This chapter provided an overview of the major historical and current issues regarding access and equity for traditionally underrepresented student populations. School counselors and school-based college counselors working toward college and career readiness for all students have a special role and responsibility. Examining social capital, advocacy, and components of school counseling programs and activities, this chapter responds to critical questions about actions and positions school counselors and school-based college counselors must take to further this important work to help all students meet their college and career goals.

Chapter Three

Career Theory and Exploration

This chapter provides a review of the fundamentals of career counseling theory. Ethical issues are discussed. Implications for work with students in K–12 settings are explored in relation to common comprehensive school counseling strategies and approaches.

CAREER THEORY AND EXPLORATION

Most school counselors completed a career course as part of their educational program. Some may have also completed advanced training or workshops on specific approaches and tools for career exploration as part of their ongoing professional development. As a supplement to those essential aspects, this chapter provides a brief review of the fundamentals of career counseling theory with the assumption that school counselors have already acquired more thorough explanations of career theory and career counseling through master's level coursework, professional development and clinical supervision, or continuing educational opportunities.

Ethical issues and various educational and informational sources are also included in this chapter, as well as implications for work with students in K–12 settings in relation to popular comprehensive school counseling models.

Career development is both a process and a consideration of contextual influences that shape careers over the life span (Niles & Harris-Bowlsbey, 2013). Career development considers roles, lifestyle, and education in relation to self and an ever evolving awareness of self. In short, career development is how we understand ourselves as we relate to the world of work. As is true with other theories of counseling, career counseling theory provides the framework for understanding the approaches, interventions, strategies, and tools counselors use as they work with people to help them better understand themselves.

Career development theory helps counselors help individuals work toward personal goals and preferred future roles and lifestyles. For school counselors, career development theory provides an important structure or guidepost for beginning to understanding the career development of children and adolescents. As school counselors work with students individually, and in large and small groups, the use of a theoretical framework helps to understand the issues at hand, shape the counseling goals and outcomes, and ground and unify the counseling approach.

Career theory provides the structure of career counseling that prevents the school counselor from offering a random, disjointed smattering of career related activities to learners. For example, while a career fair, a read aloud story on community helpers, and a Bingo game on jobs may be appropriate for elementary school students, these activities would better serve students if they were undergirded and united by a theoretical approach to career development that helps students explore who they are and their career goals and influences. Using a theoretical framework to shape the work provides a context for students' growth around issues of career counseling.

Knowledge and competence regarding career development counseling and theory is supported by the National Career Development Association's Multicultural Career Counseling Minimum Competencies (NCDA, 2009), the National Career Development Association Code of Ethics (2015), the Council for the Accreditation of Counseling and Related Educational Programs Standards (CACREP, 2016), and the American School Counselor Association (ASCA).

ASCA's "Mindsets and Behaviors for Student Success" (2014) identifies career development as one of the major areas that enhance the student learning process and create a culture of college and career readiness for all students. Moreover, the ASCA School Counselor Competencies identify career counseling theory competence as a fundamental framework a school counselor must possess. The competencies ensure that school counselors, whether new to the field or well established, are equipped to build, maintain, and enhance a comprehensive school counseling program addressing academic achievement, personal/social development, and career readiness.

Ethics in Career Counseling

The National Career Development Association (2015) Code of Ethics provides primary guidance for counselors regarding career counseling and planning. School counselors working with students on career counseling and planning issues must be mindful of several key ethical issues. Three of those issues are discussed below.

First, school counselors must always remember the ethical responsibility to recognize and affirm the dignity and worth of each individual student and family. School counselors must invest in effective counseling relationships with their students and be prepared to form collaborative relationships with students' families and communities to meet student needs and best interests. This suggests that career counseling interventions, curricula, and activities must be vetted and determined appropriate not for students in general, but for the specific students on the counselors' caseload.

Second, school counselors must be aware of and responsive to the cultural needs of students. Career development for all students occurs within a cultural context that requires effective counseling responses to all salient aspects of students' diversity including but not limited to race, ethnicity, sexual orientation, gender, socioeconomic strata, ability, and age. Culturally responsive career counseling is deeply informed by students' worldviews. Moreover, school counselors who practice culturally appropriate career counseling understand the reality of barriers rooted in injustice and discrimination and work to eliminate them.

Third, ethical school counselors select and use career assessment appropriately. Today there are many career assessments and tools available online and in commercially prepared products. School counselors must be sure they are appropriately trained to administer these tools. They must also make sure that they use and share the data from assessments and other career tools in appropriate ways. Keeping in mind the developmental status of students, school counselors must be particularly careful not to overstate, inappropriately generalize, or broadly apply career assessment results.

For a more complete review of ethics specific to career counseling, readers should consult the National Career Development Association Code of Ethics (2015).

CAREER THEORY OVERVIEW

Holland's Theory of Vocational Types

Holland's (1997) theory of types is based on the assumption that people can be characterized by their personality type or typology, and work can be characterized by its environmental type or typology. In general, people choose careers and work environments that are congruent with their interests and personality types. Implicit in this assumption are further tenets of Holland's theory that include the belief that occupation is a choice, members of an occupational group have similar personalities, and congruence between one's personality and job lead to greater levels of satisfaction, achievement, and stability. Holland's work organizes around six personality types.

The realistic personality type prefers work that is hands on and uses tools and/or machines in active, practical applications. This type tends to prefer concrete rather than abstract problems. Realistic type personalities are often described as practical, conforming, persistent, and stable, and may not be attracted to positions that require high levels of social interaction or social skill.

The investigative personality type prefers work that is observational, systematic, and analytical. Investigative types prefer to think through problems rather them act them out as realistic types do. Investigative type personalities are often described as intellectual, scholarly, curious, reserved, and introverted, and may not prefer positions that require high levels of social interaction, adventure, or repetition.

According to Holland's theory, the artistic personality type prefers work that is creative, artistic, free-flowing, and spontaneous. Artistic type personalities are often described as expressive, imaginative, independent, and intuitive, and may not be attracted to positions that require high levels of order, convention, and systematic implementation. Artistic types typically prefer to approach problems through creative expression.

The social personality type prefers work that involves training, educating, and developing others. Social type personalities prefer to face life's challenges through discussion and interactions with others. Social type personalities are often described as helpful, friendly, understanding, and humanistic. Social types may not enjoy positions that require high levels of order and work with machines or tools.

Enterprising personality types prefer work that is aimed toward attaining organizational or economic goals. Enterprising type personalities are often adventurous, persuasive, direct, and extroverted with abilities and interests in selling, persuading, marketing, and managing. Enterprising personality types usually do not favor positions that involve high levels of creativity, symbolism, and systematic analytical approaches.

The final type of Holland's theory, the conventional personality type, prefers work that is highly ordered and involves manipulation of data. Conventional personality types are described as efficient, conscientious, orderly, and practical. Conventional personality types are not usually drawn to work that demands creative, emotive engagement.

Holland's theory uses these same types to describe work environments. Congruence, as defined in the theory, therefore, is a fit between an individual's personality type and his or her work environment. Incongruence is a lack of fit between one's type and work environment. It is the interaction between a person's dispositions and the environmental conditions, or the Person-Environment fit that is a key descriptive element of Holland's work.

Differentiation, another key concept of Holland's theory, describes the level or degree of clarity in a person's personality code and the resulting predictability in career choice. For example, one student may have clearly defined, strong preferences. This student would have a highly differentiated Holland type that would point to distinct work environments and related jobs.

On the other hand, another student may express equal interest in a variety of types that overlap and are not clear-cut. For example, a student may express equal, moderate interest in artistic, social, and realistic types. This student would have a Holland profile that is undifferentiated. This student's profile would not point to a set of clearly defined work environments and jobs, thus making career choice less predictable.

Holland's theory notes that both environmental and personality typologies have a specific level of relatedness, which he described through the use of a hexagon with designated points: RIASEC. These ordered points, which stand for the first letter of each of the types (i.e., Realistic, Investigative, Artistic, Social, Enterprising, and Conventional), through proximity on the hexagon show the level of relatedness, consistency, and congruence of the types. For example, a social and artistic type in both personality and environment have more in common than a social and realistic type. For a more thorough review of the relationship among Holland types and implications for counseling, readers should consult the reference list at the end of this book.

The Self-Directed Search® (SDS, Holland, 1970) is the most popular tool counselors use to help students identify their Holland type. The SDS is a career interest test that includes questions about aspirations, activities, skills, and jobs. Responses yield a three-letter code that can be used to identify occupations and fields of study that are congruent with the test taker's personality. The assessment is available in many formats, languages, and reading levels, but it is most appropriate for students 11 and older (see Reardon & Lumsden, 2002). Many activities and approaches based on Holland's theory, however, have been developed for younger students (see Osborn, 2002).

Given the breadth of application of the theory, school counselors working with kindergarten through high school–aged students can effectively use Holland's theory to help students move toward self-awareness, differentiation, and then congruence—identifying and then connecting with congruent work roles and environments based on their personality type. Holland's theory provides an accessible, easy to understand approach for children and adolescents who are beginning to understand careers and their evolving career development (see Gottfredson & Johnstun, 2009; Niles & Harris-Bowlsbey, 2013).

One of the great advantages of Holland's theory for school counselors is that it is well researched, showing validity across both gender and race (see Morgan, deBruin, & Bruin, 2015; Rounds & Tracey, 1996; Tang, 2009). It also provides a framework that is easily understood by most children and adolescents. Moreover, the theory undergirds many of the career-based programs and tools readily accessible to today's school counselors and school systems.

One of the greatest limitations of the theory is that it does not adequately account for a number of significant influences that affect career, including job market; cultural perceptions, values, and norms; geographical boundaries; and personal factors like risk tolerance, and levels of need for convenience, satisfaction, financial security, and stability.

The theory may also lead school counselors to narrowly focus all efforts of career counseling on job searches and securing a position, and ignore the broader area of *career development* over time that is important for the healthy growth of children and adolescents. These important realities should be considered by school counselors working with students and entire school populations.

Super's Life-Span, Life-Space Theory

Super's life-span, life-space theory (see Super, 1980) takes into consideration the developmental aspect of career counseling. Super's theory situates career development as a lifelong process. Over time and in light of life experiences, one's self-concept changes and develops. As one's self-concept develops and stabilizes, so does one's ability to choose occupations that align with that developing sense of self.

In addition to recognizing that self-concept continues to develop over time, Super also recognized that individuals take on life roles that change and intersect. The many life roles Super identified include child, student, leisurite (one who engages in leisure activities), citizen, worker, parent, and homemaker. According to the theory, life roles along with environmental, situational, and personal factors affect and inform the work people do. Super's life-career rainbow provides a visual representation of the roles individuals play across their lives and the time typically spent in those roles.

School counselors can help children and adolescents understand the fluidity of life roles, as even at young ages many students today take on multiple roles given their ever changing environments, situations, and personal factors. Most elementary school counselors know of several children who regularly fill not only the student role, but move in and out of a caretaker role as needed, given a variety of family circumstances. School counselors also frequently work with high school students who are not only students, but who simultaneously take on the roles of part-time employee, teammate, child, committee member, and volunteer.

Career satisfaction, a major concept of the theory, is gained through roles that allow for self-expression and further development of the self-concept. Career maturity or vocational maturity, an additional key concept, is the similarity between one's career-related actions and one's chronological age. School counselors using Super's theoretical approach to career work with students are primarily working with the first two stages of the theory: Growth and Exploration.

The major career task of Super's Growth stage is for children and young teens to develop self-concepts as they move from play to work. During the Growth stage and the three related substages (Fantasy, Interest, and Capacity), children from birth to about 14 years of age move from career fantasies (Fantasy stage), to identifying career likes and dislikes (Interest stage), to a period where they are able to relate their own skills to specific job requirements (Capacity stage). It is important to note that the ages for this stage and all stages of the model are not fixed, as some students will be older or younger as they navigate these stages.

School counselors can support this kind of developmental progress as they observe and listen to kindergarten and first grade students talk about becoming ballerinas or firefighters and then later during the older elementary and middle school years begin to match those same professions to the actual skill sets one must possess to lead to those careers. The key roles of school counselors helping students navigate the Growth developmental stage is to help students begin to understand the world of work and sharpen and deepen students' understandings of self.

School counselors may find that their older students have reached the Exploration stage of Super's model. During this stage of career development older teens and young adults may yearn to try out careers through coursework, hobbies, shadowing, and volunteer activities. These tentative career choices are often driven by students' interests and abilities. The later parts of the Exploration stage are defined by substages where students "crystalize" a vocational preference and specify a vocational preference as their self-concept becomes relatively stable.

School counselors working with high school students navigating these Exploration substages can most benefit students by helping them solidify their sense of self. School counselors can do this by helping students learn more about life career opportunities and helping them explore job preferences through community service and engagement in short, job shadow experiences and extracurricular activities.

Constructivist and Narrative Approaches

Constructivist and narrative career approaches move away from trait and factor approaches to ones that explore memories, experiences, dreams, and themes and how those shape into authentic, individualized narratives or stories of career. These approaches aim to unearth personalized meaning and to tell and understand the story of career through an individual's lived experiences. These approaches acknowledge the importance of critical reflection and meaning-making.

Counselors using these approaches must fully respect students' authority on their own life experiences, yet offer a therapeutic relationship that contributes to their growth through honest examination of important questions, patterns of thought and behavior, and actions that help the students move toward meaningful goals and career decisions.

Savickas's (2012) life design intervention model helps counselors and their clients understand the clients' career questions and explore roles and stories. The model provides a framework for considering multiple perspectives, identifying action steps and activities, and then applying those to further development. Savickas's life intervention model may prove particularly beneficial for students of color and students from other marginalized populations in that it considers and centers multiple perspectives, values, and worldviews when considering life work goals, themes, and experiences. Lived experiences and contexts are significant using this approach. It is important to note that students of color and students from other marginalized populations can fully express and operate within culturally appropriate contexts using culturally relevant and individually meaningful measures and systems using the Savickas model. This allows constructed ideas and goals of work and career to be extremely purposeful and satisfying.

School counselors have opportunities to incorporate elements of narrative career counseling approaches with their students in small group counseling interventions and individual counseling across the K–12 continuum. Part II of this book includes examples of career counseling narrative approaches for students.

Gottfredson's Theory of Circumscription and Compromise

Gottfredson's theory of career development (1981) centers on the elimination and retention of career choices. According to the theory, over time and shaped by the interplay of an individual's cognitive growth, chronological age, and social and cultural environment, one zeros in on acceptable career alternatives and eliminates those that are not acceptable. Acceptable career alternatives are defined by interests, levels of prestige, and sex type. The model has a series of stages that individuals move through as they develop.

The first stage of Gottfredson's model is Orientation to Power and Size. During this stage, young children, typically ages 3–5, develop an understanding of occupations as adult roles. Their understanding largely comes from their observations and awareness of adults in the world around them. Given this, school counselors working with very young children should expose the children to a wide variety of adults in the world of work. Experiential and vicarious exposure to the world of work broadens children's knowledge of what is possible.

The second stage of the model is shaped by a consideration of sex roles. Between the ages of 6 and 8, in this Orientation to Sex Roles stage, children typically see occupations as "jobs for girls" or "jobs for boys." While there may be some degree of flexibility in this conceptualization of jobs, it is important for school counselors to know that students may consciously or subconsciously, appropriately or more likely inappropriately, eliminate occupations or entire fields they do not consider consistent with their sex-role preference.

Culturally competent school counselors are aware of this developmental process and can help young students in particular keep wide their perceptions of possibilities for themselves.

During the third stage of the model, 9- to 13-year-olds begin to consider social class and those occupations that meet or exceed their expectations regarding prestige and social class while disregarding occupations that do not meet their expectations in this regard. Young people in this stage may also begin to evaluate potential occupations based on their emerging sense of their academic abilities and their notions of required effort. This important third stage of development is called Orientation to Social Valuation.

Here again, culturally competent school counselors have an important role to play. Recognizing the major decisions of this stage, culturally competent counselors must stay committed to helping students become aware of and consider as wide a range of occupations as possible.

During the final stage of the model, Orientation to Unique Internal Self, older children and adolescents consider their personal interests, skills, and values to identify careers or career fields that are acceptable. During this stage, adolescents and young adults develop an ever increasing clarity about what careers align with their goals, values, and interests and begin the process of rejecting those that do not (circumscription).

Compromise may occur out of necessity as individuals work closer and closer toward their career choice. Should compromise need to occur due to the economy, shifting labor demands, family needs, or other factors, according to Gottfredson's theory, individuals first compromise alignment with their professional interests. Compromises regarding occupations aligned with a perceived level of prestige or social class are explored next. Least resistant according to the theory are career choices regarding sex-type.

Gottfredson's theory of circumscription and compromise has important implications for school counselors. It suggests that career development and awareness must begin early in schools and continue through adolescence. School counselors would be well served to work with students K–12 and help them expand their notions of the world of work in a culturally relevant context. Moreover, school counselors using this theoretical model can help students address and discover for themselves helpful or limiting notions of career circumscription and compromise.

Social Cognitive Career Theory

The social cognitive career theory (Lent, Brown, & Hacket, 2000) considers how academic and career interests develop, how educational and career choices are made, and how academic and career success is achieved. Self-efficacy (or one's beliefs about her or his abilities), outcome expectations, and goals undergird these processes. Over time career goals and choices change as one's self-efficacy, outcome expectations, and goals interface with one's performance record, affective state, vicarious experiences, and cultural dimensions.

This theory of career development may have particular interest for school counselors and their students because it is so closely tied to expectations and goals that align well with education contexts and processes. A school counselor at any instructional level would well serve her students by providing opportunities for them to expand and strengthen their abilities through direct experience and vicarious learning.

Imagine the positive experiences for students to gain levels of self-efficacy through serving as a peer buddy in academic or social school activities, or participating in internships or field trips that expose students to career roles. While typically situated solely as academic events, plugging in the school counselor and a comprehensive developmental college and career readiness curriculum can help broaden the objectives embedded in these activities and provide wonderful opportunities for students to deepen their understanding of career.

Career Counseling in Schools

The theories briefly discussed above offer school counselors a framework for beginning to understand the career development of children and adolescents. As school counselors work with individual students and develop interventions and programs for larger groups of students, career theory helps counselors more deeply understand the issues at hand, shape the counseling goals and outcomes, and ground and unify the counseling approach.

Within any appropriately selected theoretical framework, school counselors at all instructional levels can help students work toward four basic career development tasks: gain self-knowledge, explore, question, and plan. While career theory provides a necessary conceptual grounding and often suggests a specific counseling approach, school counselors should keep in mind these basic tasks of career development in K–12 settings.

The first task of school counselors is to help their students work toward self-knowledge. As school counselors facilitate students' paths through school counseling curriculum, deepening self-knowledge can and should be approached at the elementary, middle, and high school levels. School counselors working toward this career task can help students understand more fully who they are, what they value, what they believe, and how they see the world. While these understandings deepen over the life span, students at every age can have critical work and learning that focuses on self-knowledge.

The second basic career development task is exploration. Through play, community- and school-based experiences, vicarious experiences, and a host of other opportunities, school counselors can help students explore their interests, aptitudes, passions, and motivations. Again, as these evolve over a lifetime, school counselors at each instructional level have an opportunity to help students open new doors of exploration. Key to this task is school counselors' efforts to help students explore as many options as possible and not to prematurely close off any avenues of possible career exploration.

The third basic career development task is to question. School counselors are uniquely positioned and skilled to use individual, small group, and large group counseling approaches to help students ask and answer important questions about their career dreams, goals, desired future life/work balance expectations, and career needs. Kindergarteners through twelfth graders can and should be supported and prompted by school counselors to ask questions about their futures and the career paths they hope to pursue.

The final basic career development task is to plan. Perhaps the best known career development task, good planning should not occur in the absence of the other three essential tasks. As students become developmentally ready, school counselors can provide key support in helping students and their families identify career goals, gather career information, and develop and execute appropriate career plans. Career plans can take the shape of transition plans or individual learning plans or they can be more informal, such as reflection exercises or decision tree activities that are part of small group counseling or individual counseling sessions.

The second part of this book provides lessons, activities, and strategies school counselors can use to help students approach the four basic tasks of career development.

Chapter Four

Building a Solid Foundation with School-Family-Community Partnerships

This chapter explores the key role of school-family-community partnerships in college and career readiness counseling. Special emphasis is given to the ways in which these ties support and inform students' development and movement toward meeting college and career goals. Models, terms, and implications for school counselors are discussed.

SCHOOL-FAMILY-COMMUNITY PARTNERSHIPS

Few would argue the tremendous positive effects of school-family-community partnerships on students' educational and social outcomes. Many research studies have examined the value of school-family-community partnerships across grade levels and varied community and demographic variables (Epstein & Sheldon, 2016; Epstein & Van Voorhis, 2010; Henderson & Mapp, 2002).

At root, effective partnerships are two-way, collaborative relationships through which school, family, and/or community members exchange dialogue, ideas, insights, dreams, goals, supports, and resources to serve students. Partnerships support student success effectively because they bring together the multiple areas that influence and shape student development (Epstein & Sanders, 2006). When a student's home, school, and community work toward the same aims (i.e., supporting college and career readiness), learning and growth is reinforced in multiple places in multiple ways.

The American School Counselor Association position statement on "The School Counselor and School-Family-Community Partnerships" (2016) recognizes counselors' unique position to promote, facilitate, and advocate for partnerships. School counselors are well positioned to use their communication and counseling skills along with their understanding of social systems and social capital to leverage partnerships that meet the needs of students. For the benefit of students, school counselors must be willing to prioritize partnership work within the scope of comprehensive school counseling programs.

While the use of effective partnerships is key in all areas of the students' academic and social lives, partnerships may have particular relevance for areas of school counseling programming focused on college and career counseling. Importantly, emerging research suggests that low-income students and students of color may see significant benefits from school-family-community partnerships related to college and career readiness (Holcomb-McCoy, 2010).

This chapter explores the key role of school-family-community partnerships in college and career readiness counseling. Special emphasis is given to the ways in which these ties support and inform students' healthy development and attitudes toward college and career. Models, terms, and implications for school counselors are discussed.

Characteristics of Partnerships

In the world of school counseling, some of school counselors' most significant partnerships are with teachers. Many school counselors would be unable to implement important aspects of a comprehensive school counseling program without the partnership of teachers who work with them to deliver classroom guidance lessons, intervene on behalf of students, and plan and run major schoolwide activities. These partnerships are crucial. However, at times, school counselors must move beyond these inside-the-schoolhouse partnerships.

Most school counselors and individuals in school counseling preparation programs have planned K–12 school-based career fairs or classroom activities that include members of the local community, for example. Often these "partnerships" involve community members sharing what it is they do in the world of work. Over time and with some planning, these learning events at the elementary school level may go the extra step and include real work tools and opportunities for students to actually try on a firefighter's jacket or wear a chemist's goggles.

Many are also familiar with the family workshop that offers family members strategies to work with students on specific academic skills or provides information on financial planning for college. School counselors, teachers, and administrators often plan the content for these events and deliver the content through small groups and interactive sessions. Attendance at these events is bolstered by food and beverages provided by local fast food business "partners."

While helpful and indeed appreciated, these examples only touch the surface of what is possible in school-family-community partnerships focused on college and career readiness. True school-family-community partnerships go way beyond the provision of food or one-time, drop-in talks or sessions for students. True school-family-community partnerships are coordinated collaborations intentionally designed to support and promote students' growth. They are data-driven, equitable, and embody commonly shared values and goals. Effective partnerships are two-way, in that both partners' voices are valued and respected, and the relationships are *mutually* rewarding and beneficial.

Partnerships in most fields, and especially in education, take time to develop. Often during the first few months of engagement, partners are developing rapport and clarifying goals. Meaningful work tends to begin and stabilize over the first few years of a partnership. Over time, perhaps two or three years into the partnership, the work and operational processes start to become institutionalized. This is particularly important in schools and communities where, for the sake of the students, it is critical that partnerships extend beyond a single school counselor or community leader who may transfer to another geographic area or eventually work in a different capacity.

While it is true that effective partnerships must be sustainable beyond the efforts of a single person, it is also true that effective partnerships are often initiated by a key leader. A strong leader is important to the process of partnership development. Effective school counselors possess a unique set of human interaction skills that allow them to engage in effective communication and lead partnerships in the crucial beginning stages. They are also trained to facilitate relationships that operate on trust and are focused on problem solving. Importantly, school counselors are able to recognize bias in themselves and others and the ways that bias may affect goals and student outcomes.

Bias and Deficit Thinking

The ability to recognize and affectively address bias in oneself, others, and organizations is important when considering school-family-community partnerships aimed to support students' college and career readiness. It is important that the individuals in partnerships understand deficit thinking and strategically work to ensure deficit thinking and models do not become the lens through which the partnership operates.

Deficit thinking suggests that students from marginalized and underserved communities, including immigrant, low-income, and minority students do not succeed in school because of some inherent deficit, barrier, behavior, or attitude. This type of thinking is incorrect and inappropriate. It evolves into stereotypes and faulty notions, narratives, and approaches that focus on problems rather than solutions for students. Deficit thinking in education results in low expectations and low standards for students. Deficit thinking leads to actions that have real-world consequences for students and their communities.

For example, it could be deficit thinking or patterns of thought that could lead school counselors and community partners not to include technology and robotics professionals in the elementary school science fair because of the faulty belief that those professions are not "realistic" for students in a particular community. It is the same faulty thinking that could lead school personnel to not partner with a top tier university because of the belief that none of the community's students could ever attend the institution.

Strength-based Approaches

Partnerships that use strength-based approaches operate differently. Partnerships that use strength-based approaches use data and collaborative decision-making processes to set high goals for students. The partners in these relationships clearly identify problems, actively solve those problems using the strengths and assets of the student population and community, and remain flexible so that incoming data can be used to honestly evaluate and modify the approach as needed.

The benefit of operating partnerships in this manner is that a strength-based approach gives voice to the values and lived experiences of the partners. Rather than privileging a practice or approach that does not have cultural relevance, a strength-based approach assesses and pulls together that which is in the community to best meet the needs of the students.

This does not suggest that effective partnerships should never bring external or new opportunities to students. What it does suggest is that partnerships should fully use and not overlook or dismiss the resources and supports in the community. For example, to further communication competencies and college and career readiness goals, the school counselor could partner with the school's English teachers and the community liaison to invite a local spoken word poet to do a half-day workshop with eighth grade students. A follow-up community event and performance at a local coffee shop could feature some of the eighth graders as event planners, public relations personnel, hosts, performers, wait staff, and cashiers; students could simultaneously donate funds to a designated children's after-school program.

This example demonstrates the ways in which a skilled, innovative school counselor could help eighth graders gain a number of college and career readiness skills through exposure to community partners with expertise in communication, business management, accounting, performance, event planning, marketing, and hospitality. Additionally, this example alludes to the kind of mutually beneficial, affirming, and respectful relationship that is the hallmark of solid school-family-community partnerships.

Models of Partnerships

Ferguson's Model of Community Development Alliance (1999)

Partnership models provide school counselors with a framework for understanding how partnerships develop and can be effectively sustained. One such model is Ferguson's (1999) developmental model of community development alliance. This model describes tasks for each stage of development. As these issues are resolved, individuals in the partnership move to the next developmental challenge. Successful negotiation is important since failure to negotiate any particular challenge may result in lack of development and ultimate failure of the partnership.

Trust and Interest versus Mistrust and Disinterest is the first stage of the model. During this stage, the partners must determine the interest and need for partnership, explore expectations, and use the social capital that partners hold to fully understand and comprehensively approach the multiple dimensions of the issues at hand. Failure to negotiate this stage could result in a partnership ending before it truly has gotten off the ground.

School counselors navigating this stage of partnership development to further students' college and career readiness would be well served to bring multiple stakeholders to the table and provide ample opportunity and a variety of formats to hear the voices of the partners. While meetings may work to meet this aim in some communities, counselors could use informal, less structured events like coffees, student athletic games, or social events to give families and community partners a chance to meet, talk, and over time share their hopes, dreams, and goals for students and the community.

The key for this first stage is the development of trust. In order to facilitate the development of a trusting relationship, counselors must willingly commit time and interest to the lived experiences, needs, and goals of partners and the ways those intersect with the experiences, needs, and goals of students. Historical, political, economic, and societal realities including power differentials, prejudice, and oppression must be considered as they can have profound effects on the development of trusting relationships between partners.

The Compromise versus Conflict or Exit stage provides partners an opportunity to collaboratively determine appropriate goals. As school counselors work to facilitate partnerships in this second stage, they should work as cultural liaisons to overcome or eliminate cultural barriers or power differentials. It is the school counselor's unique systemic perspective that may allow her to appropriately see the strengths of schools, families, and communities as they partner to help students meet college and career readiness aims. Failure to come to a place of satisfying compromise during this stage can lead to frustration and passive dismissal or an active, deliberative exit by a partner.

School counselors should keep in mind that the compromise required in this second stage of partnership in no way suggests that standards and expectations for students should be compromised or lowered. What it does suggest is that partners should work collaboratively and compromise on the *how* of the work. High expectations for students' career and college readiness goals should be approached from a spirit of collaboration so that all partners are free to contribute from their place of strength.

The task of the third stage, Commitment versus Ambivalence, is for school, family, and community partners to dig in and overcome the obstacles that prevent sustained commitment. This stage of partnership development rests in the hard work and time that are required for productive partnerships to not only emerge but flourish. Using skills in strength-based and multicultural counseling and consultation, school counselors can become significant allies as they help school-family-community partners build strong relationships that make positive differences for students' college and career readiness.

Partnerships deepen during the Industrious versus Discouragement stage. In this stage schools, families, and communities become true allies in helping children meet college and career readiness goals. Partner roles are defined, priorities are aligned, and power differentials are mediated through mutual respect.

It would be in the Industrious versus Discouragement stage, for example, that a partnership that once provided high school students with a single field trip experience to a small community-based business could deepen and develop into a partnership that pairs business owners with a team of teachers to enhance lessons or even coteach in a particular area of expertise related to career. School-family-community partnerships in the Industrious versus Discouragement stage of development provide pathways that open the schoolhouse doors and position partners as co-contributors in the work of assisting students to meet college and career readiness aims.

In the final stage of the model, Transition versus Stagnation, partners achieve patterns of empowerment that transfer and ultimately contribute to the growth and development of the entire community. Partnerships that focus on career and college readiness and reach this advanced stage of development could affect the outcomes for an entire school district, town, or city.

Clearly this stage of partnership does not manifest overnight. Committed school counselors can, however, over the course of a career, pour themselves into partnerships that do blossom into relationships that significantly affect an entire community's students in relation to college and career outcomes. For example, when school-family-community partnerships collaboratively set goals related to improving school attendance or improving graduation rates or increasing college applications and attendance, all of which are related to college and career readiness, student achievement can soar.

Epstein et al. Model of Partnership Framework (2002)

Epstein et al. (2002) offer a framework for partnership that includes six types of involvement: Parenting, Communicating, Volunteering, Learning at Home, Decision Making, and Collaborating with the Community. Each of these types suggests different practices or actions that aim to help schools, families, and community partners work together in comprehensive, meaningful ways that promote student success.

For example, Epstein et al. (2002) identified active parent participation in school committees as a practice of Decision Making. Providing information regarding summer reading programs was identified as a practice of Collaborating with Community. Workshops served as a practice or action of the Parenting type. Each of these types of involvement could easily be used by the school counselor to further career and college readiness goals for students. Moreover, use of all six of the types of involvement identified by Epstein could better ensure that school-family-community partnerships explore the full breadth of opportunity for collaborative engagement.

A secondary school counselor focused on providing a full range of school-family-community partnership involvement regarding college and career readiness, for example, could offer Parenting workshops that offer families information on adolescent development issues that are coupled with Learning at Home techniques for talking with adolescents about college and career goals. Through a school counseling advisory board, counselors could leverage the Decision Making, Collaborating with the Community, and Volunteering types of involvement to offer a range of career exploration or internship opportunities for students. Using email, newsletters, and phone calls, counselors could keep families up to date on important college and career announcements and dates.

Partnership Functions (Bryan & Holcomb-McCoy, 2004)

In addition to understanding partnerships through types, school counselors could focus on partnership functions. A function-based model of school-family-community discussed by Byran and Holcomb-McCoy (2004) outlined nine types of collaborative functions of partnerships. These included mentoring programs, parent centers, volunteer programs, classroom assistant opportunities, home visit programs, parent education programs, business partnerships, site-based management, and tutoring programs.

Specific to the focus on college and career planning, a school counselor could use this function-based model of partnerships to lead to collaborations with fraternities and sororities, or high school seniors and middle school students to establish a mentoring program. The counselor could also work with a partnership committee to establish an information center on the school's campus, in a local library, or in a neighborhood place of worship that includes college and career information, forms, and announcements.

A crucial component of each function in these examples and beyond is the inherent inclusivity by design of a cultural authenticity and relevance. Cultural relevance is key to partnership success and is rooted in the effective operationalization of each of the partnership functions identified by Bryan and Holcomb-McCoy (2004).

Implications

Partnerships can offer schools, families, and communities meaningful and rich approaches to meet the needs of students and further their college and career readiness skills. School counselors at all grade levels are important partnership members. While they do not work in isolation, counselors' skills, knowledge of system issues, and commitment to multicultural competence can help eliminate barriers that can render partnerships ineffective and stymie the critical, multifaceted voices of partnership work that are rooted in community strengths and based in the lived experiences of community members and their students.

School counselors who understand the power of effective partnerships and the call of the ASCA position statement on school-family-community partnerships (2016) must willingly prioritize partnership work and make space for partners within the comprehensive school counseling program. Specific to college and career readiness goals within the program, school counselors should consider the following three major commitments to partnership work.

First, school counselors should commit to continuing professional development regarding partnership development, consultation, and career and college readiness competencies for K–12 students. While many school counselors receive training in these areas in their master's programs, continuing development is a necessity in order to meet the ethical standards and highest levels of professional performance.

Second, school counselors should commit to using strength-based approaches when working with partners. Strength-based approaches honor the voices, perspectives, and beliefs of partners. While there are a number of effective models and frameworks for partnerships, some of which have been discussed in this chapter, all effective models rest on relationships that are grounded in strength-based approaches. Strength-based approaches are building blocks of a trust relationship. Strength-based approaches also ensure a high level of cultural relevancy for students and their communities.

Finally, school counselors must commit to their communities and connect with individuals such as teachers and other educators, fraternity and sorority members, university faculty, business owners, and community leaders who may serve as partners. School counselors are key members of their local communities. As committed and connected community members with a great degree of social capital, school counselors who are fully engaged in community life can be good resources and strong partners who help K–12 students meet the highest levels of college and career readiness aims.

Part II

LESSONS, ACTIVITIES, AND APPROACHES FOR CAREER AND COLLEGE READINESS SCHOOL COUNSELING

Part I of this book provided a theoretical framework for understanding effective college and career counseling in a developmental context. School counselors should use this framework coupled with an *educator's paradigm* to implement an effective school-based college and career counseling program for all students K–12.

An educator's paradigm rests first and foremost on the understanding that all college and career counseling work must be developmentally appropriate for the specific learner or group of learners at hand. The following lessons have been divided by chapter into three instructional levels: elementary, middle, and high school. In many cases, the individual lessons or suggested activities have been identified for a particular grade level within the instructional levels. It is important to note that these entries are merely suggestions.

Decisions on usability and appropriateness of each presented lesson or activity must be determined based on the developmental needs and data from the specific students at hand. That is to say, any particular lesson or activity may be used with a grade level other than what is suggested if deemed appropriate by the school counselor who has thoroughly and responsibly assessed the needs and developmental levels of her students. It is very reasonable for lessons to span one or two grade levels above or below the suggested level. Also, any given lesson may not be appropriate for a particular group of students, given those students' needs.

A second important element of the educator's paradigm to which school counselors must be mindful is that any effective lesson or intervention must be culturally relevant for the students. Lesson and activity adaptations related to format, language, context, and worldview are not only encouraged but necessary so that each lesson, activity, or approach is culturally relevant for students. School counselors should partner with teachers with expertise in culturally relevant teaching if this is a skill or knowledge set the counselor does not possess.

Finally, the lessons and activities as presented should be used as a starting place for school counselors to spur their own thinking and imagination to develop, tweak, adapt, and differentiate the instruction and learning experiences presented to maximize student learning. The best classroom guidance lessons or school counseling interventions are rarely if ever the ones that are copied directly from a book or resource. Rather, the best guidance lessons or school counseling activities are those that are data driven, based on a sound theoretical framework, and shaped to meet the specific developmental, instructional, and cultural needs of the students in context.

The following lessons and activities offer school counselors a starting place to begin to construct a meaningful and developmentally appropriate comprehensive college and career counseling program for students K–12.

Chapter Five

College and Career Readiness in Elementary School

This chapter provides examples of effective college and career readiness school counseling lessons, ideas, and approaches for elementary-aged students.

ELEMENTARY SCHOOL

The elementary school years are important to college and career readiness development. These crucial years can provide the foundation necessary for career and college readiness skills and behaviors. Career development theory suggests that important milestones are met during childhood.

Super's life-span, life-space theory (1980) theory, for example, theorized about the importance of child and student roles and how in those roles children respond to environmental, situational, and personal factors while navigating the Fantasy, Interest, and Capacity stages. More discussion of Super's theory can be found in chapter 3.

Gottfredson (1981), in her theory of circumscription and compromise, also recognized important career development stages for children during the elementary school years. Gottfredson noted that children beginning around the age of three start to develop a growing consciousness of gender, social class, and prestige as they make their way through individual processes of retaining and eliminating career options.

The more recent work of Auger, Blackhurst, and Whal (2005) affirmed not only the importance of childhood as a period of career development, but also the significant role that school counselors can have in helping young children navigate early steps regarding career aspirations, expectations, and development.

The work of college and career readiness, therefore, cannot wait. Elementary school counselors have a unique opportunity to help young students begin to make connections between their growing sense of selves and their futures in career and continuing postsecondary education.

The following lessons and ideas provide elementary school counselors with a beginning roadmap for incorporating meaningful career and college readiness standards into an elementary school counseling curriculum. Importantly, when incorporating these lessons and ideas, school counselors must ground them in a developmental context that supports exploration and a growing sense of self, roles, and environments appropriate for students navigating the stages of childhood.

This kind of developmental consideration prevents a haphazard incorporation of college and career lessons here and there. Rather, it requires that the school counselor know her students collectively and individually. She must reflect upon their needs and shape the lessons and activities suggested in this chapter in a step-by-step, consistent method that meets her students where they are and helps them progress. The grade levels listed are therefore only suggested. True assessment must always be made to determine the appropriateness for any given student or student population.

Some of the lessons in this section indicate use in classroom or small counseling group settings. While these identified plans can easily be adapted to small counseling group contexts, school counselors must be sure to use them only with applications aligned with sound group counseling theory. At all times careful consideration must be given to the stage of development of the group at hand and the appropriateness of any given session plan or activity for that level of group development.

LESSON PLANS

Topic: Study Skills / Behaviors for Learning

Grade Level: K–2
Format: Large group classroom guidance lesson
Goal: Students will identify and list behaviors necessary for learning (see ASCA "Mindsets and Behaviors for Student Success," 2014; related standards M4, M6, and B-LS3)
Materials: Puppet or doll, paper, crayons
Procedure:

1. Introduce students to a puppet friend who will begin kindergarten (first or second grade) soon. Share that the puppet friend is a little nervous because she or he does not know what to expect.

2. Ask the students to help the puppet friend by telling her or him one positive thing about school. Students may say things like, you get to meet new friends, you have fun drawing pictures, you learn how to do things, you sing songs.
3. If students do not mention it, add that in school you learn new things. Ask students to tell the puppet friend some of the things they learned in school.
4. Engage the students in a conversation about what helps them learn. Focus on the behaviors and attitudes they describe that best prepare them for learning. Students may list behaviors like listening, looking at the teacher, asking for help, trying your best.
5. Discuss with students that these behaviors are important for doing good work in school. Ask them to identify the behavior that is their favorite. Ask them to share one time they demonstrated or used that behavior.
6. Invite students to draw a picture of themselves demonstrating their favorite behavior for learning to help the puppet friend remember their advice.
7. Invite students to share their pictures with the puppet friend and the class.

Assessment: Student drawings demonstrating behaviors for learning.

Topic: Study Skills and Ways of Learning

Grade Level: 3–5
Format: Large group classroom guidance lesson or small group counseling
Goal: Students will identify strategies for studying and learning new material (see ASCA "Mindsets and Behaviors for Student Success," 2014; related standards M2, B-LS4, B-SMS6)
Materials: Exit tickets
Procedure:

1. Discuss that we all have preferences regarding ways we like to study and learn new material. Some prefer to learn in groups, while others prefer to work alone. Some prefer to listen to someone talk with others about a topic, while others prefer reading about a topic. Suggest that some like to play games that help them study while others like to make flashcards. Explain that many of us learn best when we study new material in many different ways and that knowing different ways to study and learn new material helps students do better in school.
2. Ask students why it is important for students to understand the ways they learn and many ways they can study.
3. Ask students to imagine they have a social studies test coming up in two weeks. Ask them how they could prepare for the test. Chart the students' responses. Ask students the many ways they could study and learn multiplication facts. Add these responses to the chart.

4. Invite students to think silently for one minute about their own ways of approaching new material. Ask students to raise their hand when they have thought about their own preferences for learning new material and studying. Ask them to identify and share with others around them one new strategy they could use. They may use strategies listed on the class chart.
5. Invite students to complete an exit ticket on their strategies for studying. Collect the exit tickets at the conclusion of the lesson.

Textbox 5.1.   Exit Ticket

Name _____

Date _____

Three strategies or techniques I could use when I study are:

_____

_____

_____

Assessment: Exit tickets indicating strategies for studying.

Topic: Career Awareness

Grade Level: 4–5
Format: Large group classroom guidance lesson
Goal: Students will enhance their career awareness through conducting career interviews with community members (see ASCA "Mindsets and Behaviors for Student Success," 2014; related standards M4, B-SS1, B-SS3)
Materials: Chart paper or chalkboard, student notebooks, or loose-leaf paper
Procedure:

1. Allow students to brainstorm career titles. Students may benefit by listing job titles on the board or on chart paper.
2. Discuss the variety of jobs that exist and introduce the idea that each job requires different interests and skills.

3. Have children work in pairs or triads to develop five to seven interview questions that would help them learn more about any given job.
4. Chart/list the students' questions and develop a class question list. Be certain to include the following: What is your job? What do you do on a typical day? What skills do you use in your job? What interests that you have helped prepare you for your job? What advice do you have for a student who wants to do what you do when he or she gets older?
5. Discuss tips for conducting an interview and allow a few students to model good ways to ask questions. Include tips about speaking clearly, using eye contact, taking notes, thanking the interviewee.
6. Invite the students to identify one adult in their community who has a job of interest they would like to learn more about. Prepare a list of school personnel who will also be available for this activity (e.g., administrative assistant, principal, teacher, school counselor, cafeteria manager).
7. Invite students to copy the interview questions and the tips for conducting a good interview.
8. Allow students one week to complete a career interview with an adult in their community.

Assessment: Completion of questions list and identification of a career interviewee.

Topic: Career Awareness

Grade Level: 4–5
Format: Large group classroom guidance lesson
Goal: Students will state connections between interests, skills, and jobs (see ASCA "Mindsets and Behaviors for Student Success," 2014; related standards M4, B-SMS3, B-SS 1, B-SS3)
Materials: Chart paper or chalkboard
Procedure:

1. Allow volunteers to share their career interviews with the class.
2. Chart job titles, skills, and interests as the students share their interviews. Include soft skills (e.g., working well with others, creativity, initiative, flexibility) as well as skills in particular content areas (e.g., reading skills, math skills, technology skills).
3. Ask students who did not share their interviews to reread their interviews to themselves. Ask volunteers to add any skills or interests not already listed on the chart.

4. Ask students to discuss what they learned from conducting the interview and their takeaways from the chart. Allow students to come up with their own definition of skills and interests and the ways in which the two are different and related.
5. Emphasize the connection between jobs, skills, and interests. Ask students to share connections they see between jobs, skills, and interests.
6. Invite students to draw a picture of the person they interviewed.
7. Compile drawings and interview notes in a book or post them on a bulletin board in the classroom.

Assessment: Students will describe several jobs and related skills and interests.

Topic: Career Awareness

Grade Level: 4–5
Format: Large group classroom guidance lesson
Goal: Students will identify personal connections between interests, skills, and jobs (see ASCA "Mindsets and Behaviors for Student Success," 2014; related standards M4, B-SMS3, B-SS 1, B-SS3)
Materials: My Skills and Interests worksheet
Procedure:

1. Have children reflect on themes and connections from the previous lesson.
2. Review student-developed definitions of skills and interests. Ask students to share how skills and interests may help shape and inform career choice.
3. Allow students to complete My Skills and Interests worksheet.
4. Invite students to share with a partner what they learned about their personal skills and interests.
5. Invite students to complete the following 10-minute writing prompt:

   I am interested in _____. I am skilled at _____.

   These skills and interests could help me become _____ [fill in an occupation] when I get older. I believe this occupation may be a good fit for me because _____ _____.

Assessment: Student completion of My Skills and Interests worksheet and writing prompt.

My Skills and Interests

Name _____

Date _____

Table 5.1.

Skills	Interests

Careers I want to explore that may use my skills and interests:

1.

2.

3.

Topic: Career Awareness

Grade Level: 5

Format: Large group classroom guidance lesson

Goal: Students will explore career clusters and identify cluster traits (see ASCA "Mindsets and Behaviors for Student Success," 2014; related standards M4, B-LS5, B-SS1, B-SS6, B-SS7)

Materials: Computers with internet access (perhaps within the school media center)

Procedure:

1. Introduce students to the idea of a grouping or cluster by showing them pictures of items to categorize (e.g., fruit, vegetables, shoes, clothing). Discuss how similar items share traits.
2. Introduce the related concept of career clusters.
3. Inform students that all jobs that we have today fall into one of 16 career clusters.

4. Briefly list all 16 clusters and describe characteristics of each cluster. See Bureau of Labor Statistics, Career Outlook at https://www.bls.gov/careeroutlook/2015/article/career-clusters.htm#.
5. Allow students to work in small groups to explore an assigned cluster using library or media center resources.
6. Have students report on three to five interesting facts they learned about their assigned career cluster.

Assessment: Students' oral reports on career clusters.

Topic: Career Awareness / Career Walk

Grade Level: 3–5
Format: Large group classroom guidance lesson
Goal: Students will explore career clusters and identify cluster traits (see ASCA "Mindsets and Behaviors for Student Success," 2014; related standards M4, B-SS1, B-SS6, B-SS7)
Materials: List of 16 career clusters, loose-leaf paper, or student notebooks
Procedure:

1. Lead students around the school for a 10-minute silent walk. As students move around the building (inside and outside, if possible) have them take notes on all the jobs they see being done or the jobs related to what they observe (e.g., students could list a construction job or a technology job although neither worker may actually be present during the walking tour).
2. Upon return to the classroom, allow students to share their lists. Compile one long list for the class. Review the list of 16 career clusters.
3. Ask students to work in teams to place all the listed jobs in the appropriate career cluster. Explain that students must discuss their reasoning and reach consensus when they disagree about the appropriate career cluster.
4. Ask students to share their classifications. Allow students to describe any career cluster that was not visible on the walking tour and list jobs that are associated with that cluster.
5. Ask students to write a brief paragraph about the career cluster they find most interesting. Remind students to include at least three facts about the career cluster and three jobs that are associated with that cluster.

Assessment: Students' paragraphs on career cluster traits and jobs.

Topic: Study Skills / Time Management

Grade Level: 3–5
Format: Large group classroom guidance lesson
Goal: Students will develop a personal schedule and discuss the importance of time management to success (see ASCA "Mindsets and Behaviors for Student Success," 2014; related standards M1, B-LS1, B-LS3, B-SMS2, B-SMS8)
Materials: My Schedule worksheet (see figure 5.1)
Procedure:

1. Introduce the concept of time management. Explain that time management is important so that we can handle our responsibilities and complete all the things that are important to us. Explain that a schedule is one tool students can use to help with their time management.
2. Ask students to list all the things they must do between the end of the school day and the time they go to bed. Lists may include play a game, complete homework, go to soccer practice, do chores, eat dinner, free time, brush teeth, take a bath.
3. Ask the students to complete the My Schedule worksheet. Discuss the students' work and the importance of planning and using a schedule.
4. Ask students to think about the ways a schedule may help them when they are in middle school, high school, or college. Emphasize the importance of scheduling for productivity and meeting goals.

Assessment: Completion of students' schedule worksheets and participation in discussion.

Topic: College Awareness

Grade Level: 3–5
Format: Large group classroom guidance lesson or small group counseling
Goal: Students will begin to identify specific colleges and state one general benefit of college to future success (see ASCA "Mindsets and Behaviors for Student Success," 2014; related standards M4, M6, B-LS5, B-LS6, B-SS1)
Materials: Three to five athletes', public figures', school leaders', and/or music icons' pictures with colleges written on the back, large map, markers, one computer with internet access

My Schedule

Name_____

Date_____

Activity	Start Time	End Time
School		
Bed Time		Wake up at _____

Figure 5.1.

Procedure:

1. Show the students a picture of a famous athlete, public figure, or music icon. Ask the students where the individual went to college. Share the name of the college with the students if they do not know. Older students can be told the icon's college major and degree.
2. Pull up the college website using an internet search engine. Have students scan the welcome page. View a brief online tour, if available. Determine where the college is located.
3. Ask one student to place a marker for the athlete's or icon's college on a classroom displayed map.
4. As the students discover the variety of colleges their favorite athletes and music stars attended, discuss the role of college in helping them prepare for their futures. Briefly discuss the various types of colleges that are in different parts of the country. Emphasize that college provides a way to continue the learning that begins in elementary, middle, and high school. Emphasize the connection of continuing education to future success.
5. As an oral exit ticket, ask students to name one college they learned about during the lesson. Ask each student to share one way college attendance can contribute to future success.

Assessment: Students' ability to name at least one college and the benefit of attending college to future success.

Topic: Social Skills

Grade Level: K–1
Format: Large group classroom guidance lesson
Goal: Students will demonstrate noncognitive work skills (see ASCA "Mindsets and Behaviors for Student Success," 2014; related standards M6, B-LS2, B-SMS1, B-SMS2, B-SS2, B-SS6, B-SS7, B-SS9)
Materials: LEGO bricks or building blocks, drawing paper, crayons, chalkboard or chart paper
Procedure:

1. Allow students to work together in groups of three or four to build a LEGO castle for about 5 to 10 minutes.
2. Allow students to share their castles with the class. Ask the students how they worked together. Ask them what behaviors they used when working together. Have them identify what helped them work together well.

Students may say things like we took turns, nobody was too bossy, we were nice to each other, we helped each other, we said please and thank you, we shared ideas about what to build (noncognitive work skills). List the skills as the students share them. Picture cues may be used along with the written words.
3. Explain to the students that they had a job (to build a castle). Explain that they had to get along in order for the job to be completed. Explain that if they did not get along, the job would not have been completed.
4. Tell children that when they get older and work outside of school, they will have to remember the same skills they used in their groups.
5. Read aloud the student-generated list of noncognitive work skills.
6. To close the lesson, allow the students to draw a picture of themselves and their group members demonstrating one of the noncognitive work skills.

Assessment: Children's drawings of noncognitive work skills needed to complete a job.

Topic: Career Awareness

Grade Level: 2–4
Format: Large group classroom guidance lesson or small group counseling
Goal: Students increase career awareness by discussing jobs and major job functions (see ASCA "Mindsets and Behaviors for Student Success," 2014; related standards M4, B-LS7, BSS1)
Materials: Counselor-made Bingo cards (one for each student), small paper square markers
Procedure:

1. Distribute Bingo cards and small paper squares.
2. Call career clues and job titles as listed on Bingo cards. Briefly discuss each occupation or career clue as it is called. Ask students what they know about the profession. Ask students how they could learn more about that job.
3. Ask the students if they know anyone who has that particular job. Survey the class to see who would like to pursue that profession. Continue with the game.
4. At the conclusion of several rounds, ask students to complete an exit ticket listing at least two jobs of interest discussed during the session.

Sample Bingo Card

Table 5.2.

Chemist	I travel into space	Firefighter	My job demands that I am good at math	Counselor
I study ruins	Teacher	Dance therapist	Interior designer	Ophthalmologist
Banker	Locksmith	Free Space	Historian	Entrepreneur
I help children who are ill	I fix leaks in pipes	Curator	I have special skills in science	Data entry clerk
Statistician	I defend people in courts	Travel agent	Librarian	I design buildings

Assessment: Exit ticket on careers.

Textbox 5.2. Exit Ticket

Name _____

Date _____

Two careers that interest me are _____.

One strategy or technique I could use to learn more about these careers is

_____

_____

Topic: Career Awareness / Career Museum

Grade Level: K–1, and 5

Format: Large group classroom guidance lesson or schoolwide programming

Goal: Students increase career awareness through participation in a career museum (see ASCA "Mindsets and Behaviors for Student Success," 2014; related standards M3, M4, M5, B-LS2, B-SMS3, B-SS1, B-SS2, B-SS8, B-SS9)

Materials: My Dream Job worksheet, career apparel and props

Procedure:

1. Allow selected fifth grade students to explore a career of choice. Have the student complete the attached My Dream Job worksheet.
2. On the day of the career museum, invite the fifth grade students to dress in the apparel of their dream job. Allow students to include school appropriate props. If students do not have related apparel, they may create a poster with pictures of people working in their dream job.
3. As the K through first grade students move through the museum, have the older students read their career worksheet to the students. Allow the K through first grade students to ask a few questions about each profession.
4. As a closing to this lesson, allow the K through first graders to identify jobs they saw at the museum. Engage the students in a discussion of the jobs and what people in those jobs do.
5. As a closing for older students, ask the older students to share what they learned about the job they explored during the museum and two to three ways they can prepare for that future occupation.

Assessment: Completion of the summary activity.

My Dream Job

Name_____

Date_____

1. My dream career:

2. Major job tasks or roles:

3. Educational preparation and training requirements:

4. Helpful school subjects:

5. Employment opportunities and work environments:

6. Required personality traits and skills:

7. Advantages and disadvantages:

QUICK ACTIVITIES AND IDEAS

Open Access Web-based Programs—Explore open access web-based programs or websites for information and developmentally appropriate activities related to college and career readiness. These resources may be provided by the U.S. Department of Labor, private businesses or industries, or professional organizations or affiliated bodies committed to college and career readiness.

Guest Readers—Expand on a long-held tradition by inviting parents and guardians to come into primary classrooms to read a short story. Invite parents to begin story time with a brief introduction explaining their careers in a developmentally appropriate manner. A simple script can be provided to parents and guardians indicating that they share their names, their jobs, what they do in their jobs on a typical day, and the thing they love best about their jobs. As an extension of this activity, this information can be written and posted around the classroom throughout the year.

Word Walls—Use available wall space throughout the school to post vocabulary words related to college and career (use multiple languages as appropriate given the student population). Students can use these word walls to increase their knowledge of key concepts and vocabulary.

College Bulletin Board—Make a bulletin board of the teachers' pictures and their college logos or mascots. This idea can be expanded to include math standards by making a bar graph using the information.

Going to Work Day—Invite the students to dress in apparel typical of their desired profession. Encourage students to bring school approved props. Older elementary students may also complete short stories or prepare short oral presentations about their desired professions. The day can end with completion of a class bulletin board with a picture of the students in their career dress and posting of their stories.

College Day—Invite the students and teachers to dress in college apparel. Name each classroom after area colleges or universities. Prior to College Day, work with each classroom to make a poster identifying the institution's location and at least five fun facts. On College Day, allow each class to carry the poster to the auditorium for a College Day Pep Rally where each institution is recognized and plans to attend college are celebrated.

School Jobs—Develop simple, age appropriate job applications (i.e., applicant's name, desired job, reasons why you would be good at the job) for students to complete when they wish to "apply" for a classroom or school job. Applications can be developed for line leader, classroom helper, library helper, new student buddy. This idea helps students begin to understand the connection between skills and work, and the function of job applications.

Postsecondary Preparation Programs—Invite faculty and students from community postsecondary training programs to talk with students in a center format. Encourage the faculty and their students to bring hands-on activities and displays in addition to preparing to talk with the elementary school students for about 15 minutes about the careers they help prepare adults to pursue. Allow small groups of elementary school students to rotate through two to three centers during a single class period. Community-based postsecondary preparation programs including cosmetology programs, truck driving licensure programs, nurse's aide preparation programs, and technology certificate programs offer students exposure to a wide array of important career options.

Star of the Week—Many primary grade teachers use a classroom bulletin board to highlight a different student each week. Expand on this idea and increase career awareness by having students draw or cut out a picture of their future career. A quick template can be developed for this activity so that students can place their picture into a worksheet that includes an empty frame and the words "Future _____." Add this picture to each Star of the Week bulletin.

Chapter Six

Individual Learning Plans

This chapter briefly discusses individual learning plans, their use, importance, and function in a comprehensive school counseling program.

INDIVIDUAL LEARNING PLANS

Sometime after the completion of elementary school, students and their families should be introduced to individual learning plans. Individual learning plans are documents that define and give shape to a student's academic and career goals. They are fast becoming recognized as a necessary tool for developing and documenting college and career goals (Solberg, Wills, Redmon, & Skaff, 2014). Individual learning plans or ILPs are required in most states and go by many names, including four-year plans, career plans, individual career and academic plans (ICAP), personal graduation plans (PGP), or individual success plans.

Typically, ILPs include information about a student's courses, academic requirements for graduation, grades, test scores, career and interest inventory results, extracurricular activities and achievements, service learning experiences, career readiness skills documentation, goal statements, and college and career planning worksheets or activities. They track and allow for important connections between skill development, self-exploration, career exploration, and career planning (Solberg, Wills, Redmon, & Skaff, 2014). The actual ILP format can vary based on school district requirements. Many school districts, however, are moving to more standardized paper formats or using electronic formats or web-based career exploration programs to guide and store students' ILPs.

Starting in middle school or the first year of high school, school counselors should work with students and their families to help students build their ILPs. Work on ILPs is not a one-time or annual event. Rather, strong use of ILPs involves frequent exploration that allows students to revisit their plans and shape and change them as they grow, change, and gain a clearer sense of who they are and where they plan to lead their postsecondary lives.

For school counselors, the effective use of ILPs may incorporate the full range of a comprehensive school counseling program and approaches. This could include large classroom guidance activities centered on career inventories and decision-making processes, small group counseling sessions about career goals and interests, and individual student planning meetings on course selection and test score interpretation. Each of these has the potential to provide information, assessment, and documentation for students' individualized learning plans.

ILPs also provide an opportunity for counselors to ensure that the diverse needs of individual students are being addressed within a culturally appropriate framework. For example, the personalized and self-reflective work that goes into building an ILP allows the culturally competent counselor to explore with students and families the way in which students' self-determined postsecondary plans are appropriately aligned or not aligned with students' emerging worldviews, cultural values, cultural needs, and intersecting cultural identities.

The ILP is an important tool that allows school counselors to bring all of this work together for students and families so that students gain a focused, comprehensive, and personalized view of their path and self-identified college and career goals.

Chapter Seven

College and Career Readiness in Middle School

This chapter provides examples of effective college and career readiness school counseling lessons, ideas, and approaches for middle school–aged students.

MIDDLE SCHOOL

The middle school years are important to college and career readiness development. These crucial years can strengthen the foundation of college and career readiness skills and behaviors begun in elementary school. Moreover, middle school counseling programs can broaden and deepen preadolescent and early adolescent youths' awareness of career paths and opportunities.

During the middle school years, many students are eager to connect with peers and make connections between their learning in school and practical applications in the world around them. Connections and integration with their experienced lives allows them to not only better understand themselves, but also make better sense of their learning, more fully own their learning, and gain a greater sense of independence as learners. These are important growth steps for pre and young adolescents who generally range in age from 12 to 14 years.

In addition to these significant academic growth and social/emotional growth steps, career theory suggests that these students make important steps in relation to career development. Super's life-span, life-space theory (1980), for example, theorizes the importance of child and student roles and how in those roles children respond to environmental, situational, and personal factors while navigating the Growth stage and its three substages: Fantasy, Interest, and Capacity.

In particular, school counselors can help middle school students not make premature judgments about career dislikes, likes, and abilities by exposing them to as many career opportunities and experiences as possible. More discussion of Super's theory can be found in chapter 3.

Gottfredson (1981), in her theory of circumscription and compromise, also recognized important career development stages for middle school students. Gottfredson's third stage of development, Orientation to Social Valuation, suggests that students ages 9 to 13 may begin to evaluate potential careers based on self-perceived notions of who they are as learners and their academic abilities. They may also make decisions based on levels of perceived occupational prestige and social class.

The middle school years offer a unique opportunity for professional school counselors to help students navigate these important developmental milestones by providing college and career readiness school counseling programs that are fully integrated into the educational program of the school and include all appropriate school counseling delivery modalities.

With an eye on a developmental approach to middle school college and career readiness counseling, the middle school counseling program can provide an important link between the early awareness programming done in elementary school programs and the advanced and often individualized career and college readiness counseling that occurs in high schools. The following lessons and ideas provide middle school counselors with some tools and ideas for incorporating meaningful college and career readiness programming into a middle school counseling curriculum.

It should be noted that the lessons and activities suggested in this chapter should not be offered in a haphazard or random method. Rather, the lessons and activities should be shaped and tweaked based on the school counselor's knowledge of her students collectively and individually. She must reflect upon their needs and shape the lessons and activities suggested in this chapter in a step-by-step, consistent method that meets her students where they are and helps them progress. The grade levels listed are therefore only suggested. True assessment must always be made to determine the appropriateness for any given student or student population.

Some of the lessons in this section indicate use in classroom or small counseling group settings. While these identified plans can easily be adapted to small counseling group contexts, school counselors must be sure to use them only with applications aligned with sound group counseling theory. At all times careful consideration must be given to the stage of development of the group at hand and the appropriateness of any given session plan or activity for that level of group development.

LESSON PLANS

Topic: Study Skills, Time Management, and Balance

Grade Level: 6
Format: Large group classroom guidance lesson
Goal: Students discuss the importance of time management and balance to success (see ASCA "Mindsets and Behaviors for Student Success," 2014; related standards M1, B-LS1, B-LS3, B-SMS8)
Materials: My Typical Day worksheet
Procedure:

1. Introduce the concepts of time management and balance. Explain that time management and balance are important so that we can handle our responsibilities, complete all the things that are important to us, and maintain a healthy lifestyle.
2. Ask students to list all the things they must do during a 24-hour period. Encourage students to include necessities like eating, sleeping, and exercising, responsibilities like school work and chores, and things that bring them joy like playing with friends or enjoying video games.
3. Explain that a healthy life includes balance. Explain that balance does not mean that all activities get equal time, but that all are represented in a way that is good for each individual. Explain that some middle school students try to fit too much in their days and feel stressed and pressured. Explain that others do not accomplish enough during their days and may procrastinate about important assignments at school or home. Explain that proper balance allows time for all aspects of a student's life.
4. Students may want to share their own stories of balance or overplanning and procrastination. Allow them to do so while taking all necessary precautions to maintain confidentiality regarding personal issues. Follow up with individual students as needed.
5. Allow students to complete the worksheet and answer the questions independently.
6. Ask students to think about the ways balance in their lives can help them achieve their goals for high school and beyond. Ask them to list one thing they can do to maintain or achieve better balance in their daily schedules.

Assessment: Completion of students' My Typical Day worksheets and participation in discussion. *Note:* The counselor may use the assessment from this activity to begin to identify students who may benefit from small group counseling or individual counseling on effective time management and stress management.

68   Chapter Seven

My Typical Day

Name:

Period:

Date:

Directions: Create a pie chart to show how you spend your typical day. Be sure to include portions for school, sleep, eating, fun with friends, homework, exercising, practice for sports, and other activities you complete during most days.

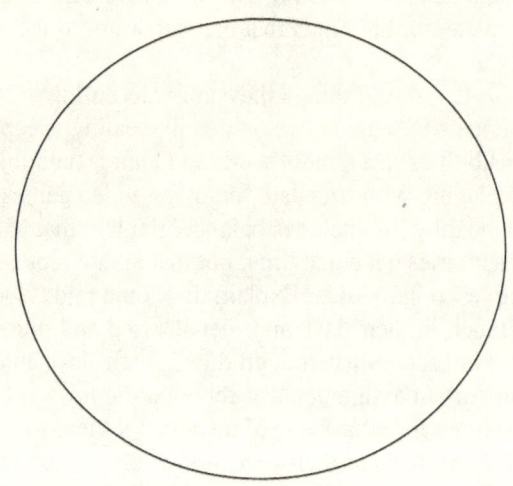

Figure 7.1.

What did you learn about how you spend your time?
Do you have a healthy balance in your typical day? What evidence supports your answer?
If you do have a healthy balance, list one way you can continue to have balance in your day.
If you do not have a healthy balance, list one thing you can do to achieve greater balance in your day.
How will a healthy balance help you meet future goals?

Topic: College and Career Readiness / Goal Setting

Grade Level: 6–8

Format: Large group classroom guidance lesson or small group counseling session

Goal: Students will discuss and identify individual academic and career goals (see ASCA "Mindsets and Behaviors for Student Success," 2014; related standards M2, M5, B-SMS5, and B-LS7)

Materials: Chart paper, markers, My Goals worksheet

Procedure:

1. Introduce the idea that attitudes and behaviors shape outcomes. Ask students to brainstorm a rationale for this connection. Ask students to think about the attitudes and behaviors that lead to the outcome of academic and career success. Some suggestions could include spending time studying, completing homework, exploring extracurricular activities, joining a school club, reading about a career field, and valuing doing well in school.
2. Distribute chart paper and markers to small groups of students. Allow students to work in small groups to identify and list behaviors and attitudes that help lead to academic and career success. Each category should include at least five behaviors or attitudes.

Table 7.1.

Attitudes and Behaviors for Academic Success	Attitudes and Behaviors for Career Success

3. Allow each group to share their lists with the other students. Note similar ideas and themes among the students' lists. Discuss the ways in which the students' two lists connect or are identical. Explain that many of the behaviors and attitudes that lead to academic success are also important for career success (e.g., good attendance, working hard, getting along with others, asking questions).

4. Emphasize the connection between school or academic behaviors and attitudes the students engage in today and their future behaviors and attitudes in careers.
5. Invite the students to individually identify one behavior or attitude from each area (i.e., academic success and career success) that is important to them and one they would like to strengthen. Explain that these general behaviors and attitudes can be made specific to address an individual's needs.
6. Talk with students about goal setting. Share that strong goals are clear, specific, achievable, and measurable. Share the following formula for goals:

   I will _____ (specific behavior or attitude) by _____ (how) for (or within) _____ (time line or frequency).

   Example: I will <u>raise my grades in science by 10 points</u> by <u>attending the afterschool homework club</u> for <u>one day each week for the rest of the second grading period</u>.

   Example: I will <u>learn three things about what it takes to be a fashion designer</u> by <u>finding two articles online and reading them</u> within <u>the next two weeks.</u>

7. Invite students to write one goal for academic success and one goal for career success using the attached worksheet. They may use the behaviors and attitudes for success generated during the first part of the lesson as inspiration for their own specific goals. Review progress toward goals during the next group or classroom session.
8. Aligned with a narrative approach to career counseling, when using a small group counseling approach, school counselors may help students extend this activity to include a written exploration of what their possible future selves can be in career if the above goals are realized. As appropriate, the counselor can help students begin to understand the meaning they have ascribed to their dreams about career through the stories they have created.

Assessment: Completion of the My Goals worksheet and review of progress.

My Goals

Name:

Period:

Date:

A goal must be:

- Clear
- Specific
- Achievable
- Measurable

Goals can be written using the following template.

I will _____ (behavior or attitude) by _____ (how) for (or within) _____ (time line or frequency).

Write one personal goal for your academic success. Is the goal clear, specific, achievable, and measurable?

_____

_____.

Write one personal goal for your career success. Is the goal clear, specific, achievable, and measurable?

_____

_____.

Topic: Self-Awareness, Interests, and Abilities

Grade Level: 6–8

Format: Large group classroom guidance lesson or small counseling group session

Goal: Students will identify personal long- and short-term career goals (see ASCA "Mindsets and Behaviors for Student Success," 2014; related standards M2, M4, B-LS7, and B-SS1)

Materials: Drawing paper, colored pencils

Procedure:

1. Share with students that they will spend the next 10 minutes imagining their future.
2. Ask students to center themselves and sit in a relaxed position. Invite them to close their eyes if they are comfortable doing so.
3. When students are settled, ask them to imagine that they are 25 years old. Ask them to visualize themselves. What are they wearing? Where do they live? Who is around them?
4. Explain that they are headed to work in a job they feel good about and makes them proud. Recognize that some students may have difficulty with this visualization and may need further prompts or time to imagine themselves in a future career.
5. When students are able to visualize themselves, ask them to think about the following: Where are they going? What time of day is it? How are they getting to work? What do they do? Do they work with others? Do they work by themselves? What is their work environment like? Are they working inside? Are they working outside?
6. Ask the students to imagine themselves working at their job for a few minutes. Allow the students to visualize their job for two to three minutes in silence. Invite them to imagine themselves moving through their work day.
7. If adapting and using this plan within a small group counseling context, allow students to adequately and safely process their feelings as they move through the visualization. Leave ample time for reflection and processing. Ask students to consider the meanings they attribute to their visualizations and the associated emotional responses. Keep in mind that this portion of the plan (step 7) should only be done in a small group counseling context. This deeper level of work cannot be appropriately tapped in a classroom setting.
8. Ask students to imagine themselves leaving their work and feeling great about their day. After a pause, ask students to open their eyes when ready.

9. Ask students to share with a neighbor what they experienced during the visualization activity. What was their job? What did they do during the day? What did they enjoy most about the imagined work day? What skills did they demonstrate? What attitudes did they have?
10. Ask students to identify the skills and attitudes that they demonstrated in their imagined career future. Ask students why those particular skills or attitudes were important to them in their future. Emphasize the connection between skills, attitudes, and future outcomes.

Table 7.2.

Skills Necessary for My Future	Attitudes Necessary for My Future

11. Recalling the elements of goals (see previous lesson), ask students to write a personal goal that will lead to mastery or acquisition of at least one skill and one attitude on their list. Discuss the importance of short-term goals that can typically be accomplished in hours, days, or weeks, and long-term goals that typically take months or years to accomplish. Discuss the connection between short-term goals as stepping stones to long-term goals.
12. Allow students to share their goals with the group. As students share, ensure the goals are clear, specific, achievable, and measurable. Ask students to identify if their goal is long term or short term. Invite students to develop at least one short-term and one long-term goal related to their future career.
13. Invite students to create a poster or picture that includes a drawing of their future selves and their short-term and long-term goals. Invite the students to keep their posters or pictures in their notebooks to remind them of their path toward their future career.

Assessment: Completion of drawings with appropriate short-term and long-term goals listed.

Topic: Career Awareness—Entrepreneurship

Grade Level: 7–8

Format: Large group classroom guidance lesson

Goal: Students will discuss entrepreneurship to expand their career awareness (see ASCA "Mindsets and Behaviors for Student Success," 2014; related standards M4, B-SS1, B-SS6, B-LS7 and B-SS7)

Materials: Pictures and stories on famous entrepreneurs, exit tickets

Procedure:

1. Introduce the students to the concept of entrepreneur and entrepreneurship. Students may offer definitions or examples.
2. Share the story of a few famous entrepreneurs like Henry Ford, Oprah Winfrey, Serena Williams, Walt Disney, Beyoncé, Magic Johnson, and Bill Gates. Modify this list to include local entrepreneurs or individuals who are particularly well known to the students. This discussion can be

---

Exit Ticket

Name_____

Date_____

Grade_____ Period_____

An entrepreneur is _____.

One skill, behavior or attitude that helps entrepreneurs be successful is

_____

One behavior, attitude or skill I have that is necessary for entrepreneurship is

_____

At this time I am or I am not interested in being a future entrepreneur because

_____

_____.

Figure 7.2.

enhanced with library or media center resources including pictures, books, and video clips.
3. Discuss entrepreneurship as a career option. Discuss the ways entrepreneurship meets community needs and provides vital services or products.
4. Ask students to break into small groups to brainstorm skills and traits necessary to be a successful entrepreneur. Allow each small group to share its list of skills and traits. Highlight content skills as well as noncognitive factors like persistence, creativity, problem solving, help seeking, and flexibility.
5. Ask students to complete the exit ticket and reflection on entrepreneurship as a career opportunity.

Assessment: Student completed exit tickets.

Topic: Career Awareness—Entrepreneurship

Grade Level: 7–8
Format: Large group classroom guidance lesson
Goal: Students explore entrepreneurship as a career option through a business plan activity (see ASCA "Mindsets and Behaviors for Student Success," 2014; related standards B-LS1, B-LS2, B-LS8, B-SS2, B-SS6, and B-SS7)
Materials: Business Plan worksheet
Procedure:

1. Review the concepts of entrepreneur and entrepreneurship.
2. Think about popular kids' products like fidget spinners, video games, or snack foods. Explain that before these products got to the homes of boys and girls, they were ideas in the heads of entrepreneurs.
3. Explain that strong entrepreneurs begin with a great plan that describes the most important elements of a product or service:
   - Name
   - Description
   - Marketing/advertising strategy
   - Costs
4. Tell students they will have two class periods to work in teams to develop a basic business plan. Discuss strategies for good team work. Place students in groups and distribute the Business Plan worksheet to each student.
5. Over two class periods allow students to complete the Business Plan worksheet. Encourage students to develop a product demo or picture of the product or service, if possible.

6. During the final class period allow students to share their basic business plans orally with the class.
7. As a summary, discuss what students learned about entrepreneurship and the skills and processes necessary for successful entrepreneurship.
8. As an extension of this lesson, selected students can meet with local entrepreneurs to learn about their process of planning for their business.

Assessment: Student completed business plans.

Business Plan

Team Members/ Business Partners' Names:

Date:

Product Information

Product or Service Name:

Product or Service Description:

Product Marketing and Advertising

Who will buy the product or service?

Why will people want the product or service? What makes it special?

How will the product or service will be advertised?

Costs

A. How much will it cost to make the product or service?

B. What other costs will the business have (for example, think about materials, and pay for workers)?

C. What will be the sale price of the product or service?

D. How much profit can be made on the product?

(C=Product sale price) - (A+B =Cost to make product and other costs) = Profit

Figure 7.3.

Topic: Study Skills and Ways of Learning

Grade Level: 6

Format: Large group classroom guidance lesson or small group counseling session

Goal: Students will identify multiple study strategies (see ASCA "Mindsets and Behaviors for Student Success," 2014; related standards M2, B-LS4, B-SMS6)

Materials: Exit tickets

Procedure:

1. Discuss that we all have preferences regarding ways we like to study and learn new material. Some prefer to learn in groups, while others prefer to work alone. Some prefer to talk with others about a topic, while others prefer reading about a topic. Suggest that some like to play games that help them study while others like to make outlines or flashcards.
2. Explain that many of us learn best when we study new material in many different ways and that knowing different ways to study and learn new material helps students do better in school.
3. Ask students why it is important for them to know multiple ways to learn new material and to study.
4. Invite students to think silently for one minute about strategies they have used to study or learn new material. Suggest that the students think about a time they performed well on a school project or test. Ask them how they prepared. After a time of silent reflection, ask the students to discuss ways they studied in small groups.
5. Challenge the small groups to make a list of various ways a sixth grader could study for a test or learn new material. Examples could include: have a friend ask you questions, make flashcards, read and reread the material, try to teach the material to a friend, make an outline, and so on.
6. Invite students to present their lists to the entire class. Have the students complete an exit ticket on strategies they plan to use to study or learn new material this week. Collect the exit tickets at the conclusion of the lesson.

Assessment: Exit tickets indicating two strategies to study or learn new material this week.

Exit Ticket

Name_____

Date_____

Grade_____ Period_____

Two strategies or techniques I will use this week to study are:
_____
_____

I plan to use these strategies when _____
_____

Figure 7.4.

Topic: Career Awareness

Grade Level: 6–7
Format: Large group classroom guidance lesson
Goal: Students will enhance their career awareness through conducting career interviews with community members (see ASCA "Mindsets and Behaviors for Student Success," 2014; related standards M4, B-SS1, B-SS3)
Materials: Chart paper or chalkboard, student notebooks, or loose-leaf paper
Procedure:

1. Allow students to brainstorm career titles. Students may benefit by listing job titles on the board or on chart paper.
2. Discuss the variety of different jobs that exist and introduce the idea that each job requires different interests and skills.
3. Have students work in pairs or triads to develop 7 to 10 interview questions that would help them learn more about any given job.
4. Chart/list the students' questions and develop a class question list. Be certain to include the following: What is your job? What do you do on a typical day? What skills do you use in your job? What interests do you

have that helped prepare you for your job? What advice do you have for a student who wants to do what you do when he or she gets older?
5. Discuss tips for conducting an interview and allow a few students to model good ways to ask questions. Include tips about speaking clearly, using eye contact, taking notes, thanking the interviewee.
6. Role-play a student asking an interviewee about her or his job using some of the questions the class developed.
7. Emphasize the demonstrated tips for conducting a good interview.
8. Invite the students to identify one adult in their community who has a job of interest they would like to learn more about. Prepare a list of school personnel who will also be available for this activity (e.g., administrative assistant, principal, teacher, school counselor, cafeteria manager).
9. Invite students to copy the interview questions and the tips for conducting a good interview.
10. Allow students one week to complete an interview with an adult in their community.

Assessment: Completion of questions list and identification of a career interviewee.

Topic: Career Awareness

Grade Level: 6–7
Format: Large group classroom guidance lesson
Goal: Students will state connections between interests, skills, and jobs (see ASCA "Mindsets and Behaviors for Student Success," 2014; related standards M4, B-SMS3, B-SS 1, B-SS3)
Materials: Chart paper or chalkboard
Procedure:

1. Allow volunteers to share a summary of their career interviews with the class (see previous lesson).
2. Chart job titles, skills, and interests as the students share their interviews. Include soft skills or noncognitive skills (e.g., working well with others, creativity, initiative, flexibility) as well as skills in particular content areas (e.g., reading skills, math skills, technology skills).
3. Ask students who did not share their interviews to reread their interview notes to themselves. Ask volunteers to add any skills or interests not already listed on the chart.
4. Ask students to discuss what they learned from conducting the interview and their takeaway from the chart. Allow students to come up with their

own definition of skills and interests and the ways in which the two are different and related.
5. Emphasize the connection between jobs, skills, and interests. Ask students to share connections they see between jobs, skills, and interests.
6. Ask students to complete a one- to two-page paper or presentation on their interview, the connection between jobs, skills, and interests, and what they learned or liked best about completing the interview.
7. Share papers or presentations the following week. Collaborate with an English teacher for integration with communication standards and class grades, as appropriate.

Assessment: Students will describe several jobs and related skills and interests in writing or through oral communication.

Topic: Career Awareness

Grade Level: 6–7
Format: Large group classroom guidance lesson
Goal: Students will identify personal connections between interests, skills, abilities, and jobs (see ASCA "Mindsets and Behaviors for Student Success," 2014; related standards M4, M5, B-LS1, B-LS9, BSMS3, B-SS1)
Materials: My Skills and Interests worksheet
Procedure:

1. Ask students to reflect upon themes and connections from the previous lesson.
2. Review definitions of skills, abilities, and interests. Ask students to share how skills, abilities, and interests may help shape and inform career decision making and career choice. Explain that an important part of adolescence is exploring and learning about one's own skills, abilities, and interests. Explain that we learn about our skills, interests, and abilities by trying new things. Discuss the importance of being open to experiences and learning.
3. Allow students to complete My Skills and Interests worksheet. Explain that the worksheet represents where students are today, and that it can and often will change over time.
4. Invite students to share with a partner what they learned about their personal skills, abilities, and interests, as they stand today.
5. Invite students to complete the following 10-minute writing prompt:

I am interested in _____. I am skilled at _____. I have _____ ability. These skills, interests, and abilities could help me become a _____ (fill in an occupation) when I get older. I believe this occupation may be a good fit for me because _____. I also understand that over time my skills, abilities, and interests may _____. As I gain new skills, abilities, and interests I may want to explore _____ career options.

Assessment: Student completion of the My Skills and Interests worksheet and writing prompt.

My Skills and Interests

Name_____

Date_____

Table 7.3.

Skills	Interests	Abilities
Right now, I have good skills in: 1. 2. 3.	My interests today are: 1. 2. 3.	So far, I have the ability to: 1. 2. 3.

Careers I want to explore that may use my current skills, abilities, and interests:

1.

2.

3.

Topic: Career Awareness

Grade Level: 6–7

Format: Large group classroom guidance lesson

Goal: Students will explore career clusters and identify cluster traits (see ASCA "Mindsets and Behaviors for Student Success," 2014; related standards M4, B-LS5, BSS1, BSS6, and BSS7)

Materials: Computers with internet access (perhaps within the school media center)

Procedure:

1. Introduce students to the idea of a grouping or cluster by showing them pictures of items to categorize (e.g., fruits, vegetables, shoes, and clothing). Discuss that similar items share traits.
2. Introduce the related concept of career clusters.
3. Inform students that all jobs that we have today fall into one of 16 career clusters.
4. Briefly list all 16 clusters and describe characteristics of each cluster. See Bureau of Labor Statistics, Career Outlook at https://www.bls.gov/careeroutlook/2015/article/career-clusters.htm#.
5. Allow students to work in small groups to explore clusters using library or media center resources.
6. Have students work in groups of two to three to prepare a PowerPoint presentation on their assigned career cluster. Encourage students to include a description of the cluster, job titles, typical wages, projected need or job openings, and required education and/or training.
7. Allow students to share their presentations during the next session.

Assessment: Students' PowerPoint presentations on career clusters.

Topic: College Awareness

Grade Level: 8

Format: Large group classroom guidance lesson or small group counseling session

Goal: Students will begin to identify specific colleges and state one general benefit of college to future success (see ASCA "Mindsets and Behaviors for Student Success," 2014; related standards M1, B-LS1, B-LS3, B-SMS2, and B-SMS8)

Materials: Pictures of celebrities, athletes, and music icons with colleges and majors written on the back (icons could include Dewayne "The Rock" Johnson, University of Miami, Bachelor's in General Studies; Gabrielle Union, UCLA, Bachelor's in Sociology; J. K. Rowling, Exeter University,

Bachelor's in French and Classical Studies; Jerry Seinfeld, Queen's College, Bachelor's in Theater and Communication; John Legend, University of Pennsylvania, Bachelor's in English; Ludacris, Georgia State University, Bachelor's in Music Management; Oprah Winfrey, Tennessee State University, Bachelor's in Speech and Drama; and many others), class map, markers, one computer with internet access

Procedure:

1. Show students pictures of three to five famous celebrity, athlete, or music icons. Ask the students where the individual went to college. Share the name of the college with the students if they do not know it. Share the icon's college major and degree.
2. Pull up the college website using an internet search engine. Have students scan the welcome page. View a brief online tour, if available. Determine where the college is located.
3. Ask one student to place a marker for the icon's college on a classroom displayed map.
4. As the students discover the variety of colleges their favorite celebrities, athletes, and music stars attended, discuss the role of college in helping them prepare for their futures. Briefly discuss the different types of colleges or universities that are in various parts of the world. Emphasize that these institutions provide a way to continue the learning that begins in elementary, middle, and high school. Emphasize the connection of continuing education to future success.
5. Share your college, major, and degree. Share the college information for selected teachers and administrators in the building. Explore college websites as time allows.
6. As an oral exit ticket, ask students to name one college they learned about during the lesson. Ask students to identify the college or major or degree that interested them most during the class discussion and why. Ask each to tell one way college attendance can contribute to future success.

Assessment: Students' ability to name at least one college; a college and major or degree of interest, and the benefit of attending college to future success.

Topic: High School Graduation Requirements

Grade Level: 8
Format: Large group classroom guidance lesson
Goal: Students will become familiar with high school graduation requirements (see ASCA "Mindsets and Behaviors for Student Success," 2014; related standards M3, B-SMS10)
Materials: Exit tickets

Procedure:

1. Introduce high school transition to students. Discuss skills and attitudes needed for successful transition. Emphasize strengths students possess that will contribute to their high school success.
2. Discuss graduation requirements. Use online resources and/or printed materials to aid the discussion on requirements for graduation.
3. Emphasize required credits or course counts in a four-year plan. Discuss electives and optional courses of study.
4. Introduce tests and required assessments. Share a typical testing schedule (during which grade the assessments are taken) and general information about the tests.
5. Discuss other appropriate graduation requirements like community service.
6. Discuss diploma and certificate options.

Assessment: Completion of exit ticket.

Exit Ticket

Name:

Period:

Date:

List two skills or traits that will support your successful transition to high school

How many credits or courses are needed in order to graduate?

    How many credits or courses in English?

    How many credits or courses in math?

    How many credits in science?

    How many credits in social studies?

What is an elective?

    What is an example of an elective?

What assessments must be passed in order to graduate?

Figure 7.5.

Topic: Social Skills

Grade Level: 6

Format: Large group classroom guidance lesson

Goal: Students will demonstrate noncognitive work skills (see ASCA "Mindsets and Behaviors for Student Success," 2014; related standards M6, B-LS2, B-SMS1, B-SMS2, B-SS2, B-SS6, B-SS7, and B-SS9)

Materials: LEGO bricks, drawing paper, crayons, chalkboard, or chart paper

Procedure:

1. Allow students to work together in groups of three to four to build a LEGO "spectacular creation" for about 10 to 20 minutes.
2. Allow students to share their "spectacular creations" with the class. Ask the students how they worked together. Ask them what behaviors they used when working together. Have them identify what helped them work together well. Students may say things like we brainstormed ideas, nobody was bossy, we listened to each other, we did not criticize each other, we were polite, we showed respect, we shared our ideas (noncognitive work skills). List the skills as the students share them.
3. Explain to the students that they had a job (to build a spectacular creation). Explain that they had to work together as a group in order for the job to be completed. Explain that if they did not work together and collaborate, the job would not have been completed.
4. Explain to the students that these same skills will help them as they enter the world of work. Explain that some employers identify these essential skills as noncognitive work skills.
5. Read aloud the student generated list of noncognitive work skills.
6. To close the lesson, allow the students to draw a picture of themselves and their group members demonstrating one of the noncognitive work skills and to write one paragraph about the ways the skill helped them complete the job at hand.

Assessment: Students' drawings and paragraphs on noncognitive work skills needed to complete a job.

QUICK ACTIVITIES AND IDEAS

Open Access Web-based Programs—Explore open access web-based programs or websites for information and developmentally appropriate activities related to college and career readiness. These resources may be provided by the U.S. Department of Labor, private businesses or industries, or professional organizations or affiliated bodies committed to college and career readiness.

College Bulletin Board—Make a bulletin board of teachers' pictures and their college logos or mascots. This idea can be expanded to include a number of math standards by allowing students to design a survey instrument to gather the college information. After gathering the data, students can analyze it and discover the best ways to present the data on a school bulletin board.

Word Walls—Use available wall space throughout the school to post vocabulary words related to college and career (use multiple languages as appropriate given the student population). Students can use these word walls to increase their knowledge of key concepts and vocabulary.

College Visit—Arrange for eighth grade students to take a walking tour of a local college. The tour could be led by college students to add a greater degree of connection for the middle school students. Be sure to include a tour of a classroom space, a science laboratory, a dorm, and the athletic facilities. If possible, arrange for the students to eat in the dining hall. Close this activity with an opportunity for students to reflect on the possibility of college attendance for their own futures and the steps needed to get to and through college successfully.

College Day—Invite the students and teachers to dress in college apparel. Name each classroom after area colleges or universities. Prior to College Day, work with each classroom to make a poster identifying the institution's location, important facts, and general admission criteria. On College Day, allow each class to carry the poster to the auditorium for a College Day Pep Rally where each institution is recognized and plans to attend college are celebrated.

First Job Opportunities—Invite local employers who have a strong record of offering teens volunteer experiences and job opportunities to come to an evening workshop for students and their families. Allow the employers to talk with students and their families about the skills, behaviors, attitudes, and steps necessary for students to be successful in their first job or volunteer work experience. Hands-on components of the workshop could include reviewing a work permit, filling out a work application, and participating in interview processes. Begin planting seeds with students and families about opportunities for student employment that may be available in the years to come.

Postsecondary Preparation Programs—Invite faculty and students from community postsecondary training programs to talk with students in a center format. Encourage the faculty and their students to bring hands-on activities and displays in addition to preparing to talk with the middle school students for about 15 to 20 minutes about the careers they help prepare adults to pursue. Allow small groups of middle school students to rotate through two to three centers during a single class period. Require students to take notes on each session attended. Community-based postsecondary preparation programs, including those for cosmetology, truck driving, nurse's aide, and technology certification, offer students exposure to a wide array of important career options.

Financial Aid Workshop—Invite students and their families to an evening or weekend program that overviews general college costs and considerations and introduces basic financial aid information. If possible, invite a local university financial aid officer or high school counselor to present and answer student and family questions. Provide a resource packet and dinner to workshop attendees.

Success Mentors—Pair selected sixth graders with selected seventh or eighth grade success mentors. Mentors and mentees should meet at least one time per week for the first few weeks of school (ideally this would be a one- to two-month experience). This success mentor program will help the sixth grade mentees manage the transition to middle school. The experience will help the seventh and eighth grade mentors gain and strengthen noncognitive skills (e.g., social skills, cooperation, focus, persistence, organizational skills, commitment) that are necessary for success in career and college. The success mentees and their mentors can celebrate at the end of the first marking period with a brief awards ceremony and pizza party.

Chapter Eight

College and Career Readiness in High School

This chapter provides examples of effective college and career readiness school counseling lessons, ideas, and approaches for high school–aged students.

HIGH SCHOOL

Traditionally, the high school years have played the central role in school counseling college and career readiness programs. As suggested in this book, however, the high school years are an important continuation of a college and career readiness school counseling program that begins in elementary school.

As high school students move through adolescence, most are beginning to gain a fuller understanding of their strengths, skills, and abilities. This increasing sense of self offers a wonderful opportunity for school counselors to work along with educational partners, school communities, and importantly, high school students and their families to help young people make sound choices in their academic and extracurricular lives that set them up for a host of postsecondary options including college and the global job market.

High school also provides an opportunity for students to deeply understand the connections between lifelong learning and the other spheres of their present and future lives (e.g., social, physical, and mental well-being). Indeed, healthy attitudes about career as a life-span construct as opposed to securing one specific job can and should deepen in high school.

Developmentally, high school students are continuing periods of rapid change. As their bodies are progressing through physical growth spurts that may have begun a few years earlier, many are also experiencing significant cognitive developments as their abilities to reason and think abstractly increase. These cognitive developments are significant for college and career readiness work because they allow the students between the ages of 14 and 18 to be able to reflect on choices and set goals for themselves that are based on a variety of complex considerations including assessment of skills, strengths, and goals.

High school students also face a variety of stressors. These include grades and academic performance, high stakes testing, parental and peer pressures, and social interaction issues including social media, relationships, sex, and alcohol and other drug use. Typically, school counselors work with students to understand and navigate these issues through the comprehensive school counseling program frameworks for personal and social counseling, not covered in this book. These stressors may, however, specifically affect a student's college and career readiness and therefore must be integrated into a full exploration of college and career readiness curriculum at the high school level.

For example, discussion of the ways one's social media profile can affect college and career application processes with high school students is an important topic. Healthy ways to cope with and manage stress during the college application process or the first job interview experience also takes on a level of significance that is crucial for school counselors to explore with students through the college and career readiness curriculum.

While peers remain important to adolescents 14 to 18 years old, as students mature they also strengthen their appreciation and valuing of significant adults, including family members, school counselors, teachers, and mentors. Given this, school counselors must note the importance of their students' peer influences when considering college and career readiness tasks and also the influences and expectations of students' significant adults. School counselors must consider all of this while primarily keeping the needs and expectations of their student clients in mind.

The cognitive and psychosocial development of older adolescents works hand in hand with Super's conceptualization of the Exploration stage of career development. During this stage of development, older adolescents gain a stronger sense of self and explore identified vocational preferences through coursework, extracurricular activities, service opportunities, and part-time jobs. School counselors can help high school students navigate this period of development by helping them gain a clearer understanding of self and encouraging them to open and not close doors to future opportunities. More discussion of Super's theory can be found in chapter 3.

Related to this, social cognitive career theory (Lent, Brown, & Hacket, 2000) holds key understandings for older adolescents as they develop beliefs about their self-efficacy. The high school years provide a good opportunity for school counselors to help students understand their abilities, outcome expectations, and goals and the ways those dimensions interact with thoughts about career.

Using Gottfredson's (1981) theory of circumscription and compromise as a framework to understand high school students' development, school counselors would appreciate that adolescence is a time when students consider their interests, skills, and values as they enter the Orientation to Internal, Unique Self stage. Here, sophisticated understandings of the intersectionality of identities may inform students' thinking, and ultimately, their thoughts about postsecondary plans and career.

The high school years are a continuation of the college and career program school counselors offer as part of a comprehensive school counseling program. Grounded by career theory, high school programs allow students to deepen their understandings of who they are and sharpen their goals for postsecondary opportunities. More than ever, this kind of life-span approach is needed. Using this kind of contextual approach, college and career readiness work moves beyond a checklist of activities to an integrated, K–12 approach.

An integrated, developmental consideration prevents a haphazard incorporation of college and career lessons here and there. Rather, it requires that the school counselor know her students. She must reflect upon their needs and shape the lessons and activities suggested in this chapter in a step-by-step, consistent method that meets her students where they are and helps them progress. True assessment must be made to determine the appropriateness of these suggested lessons and approaches for any given student or student population.

Some of the lessons in this section indicate use in classroom or small counseling group settings. While these identified plans can easily be adapted to small counseling group contexts, school counselors must be sure to use them only with applications aligned with sound group counseling theory. At all times careful consideration must be given to the stage of development of the group at hand and the appropriateness of any given session plan or activity for that level of group development.

Topic: Pregraduation Needs Assessment

Grade Level: 9–12

Format: Large group classroom guidance lesson

Goal: Students will indicate their understanding and completion of major tasks required for a successful transition to life beyond high school (see ASCA "Mindsets and Behaviors for Student Success," 2014; related standards M4, B-LS7, B-SMS3, B-SS1, B-SS9)

Materials: Needs assessment

Procedure:

1. Introduce the role of the high school counselor and the many ways school counselors help students prepare for college and career.
2. Distribute the needs assessment to each student. Explain that the students' responses will help you, the other counselors, and their teachers plan and meet their needs through classroom guidance lessons, small group counseling sessions, and individual planning meetings.
3. Explain that there are no right or wrong answers.
4. Distribute the survey and allow students to complete it.
5. Discuss your plan for follow-up as appropriate.

Assessment: Completed needs assessments.

College and Career Readiness Needs Assessment

Name _____

Date _____

Period _____

Directions: Please indicate your understanding of each of the following using the key:

Textbox 8.1.

1 = I do not know anything about this

2 = I have heard about this, but do not really understand it

3 = I have a few questions, and need help getting started on this

4 = I understand this, and have started making progress

5 = I completely understand this, and have completed this as required given my needs

---

1. I have completed my program of study for all years of high school. _____
2. I know the test or assessment requirements for graduation from high school. _____
3. I have identified my skills and interests. _____
4. I have identified extracurricular activities that match my interests. _____
5. I participate in extracurricular activities that match my interests. _____
6. I know how to effectively manage stress. _____
7. I know how to work collaboratively with my peers. _____
8. I know how to effectively communicate with peers and adults. _____
9. I use effective decision-making strategies to determine career goals that are best for me. _____
10. I have identified my career goals. _____
11. I know what it takes to reach my career goals. _____
12. I have selected programs or colleges that will help me meet my career goals. _____
13. I know the test or assessment requirements for my desired postsecondary program or college admission. _____
14. I have taken the test or assessment required for admission for my desired postsecondary program or college. _____
15. I am knowledgeable about the application process for programs or colleges that will help me meet my career goals. _____
16. I have applied to programs or colleges that will help me meet my career goals. _____
17. I understand the basics of how to pay for postsecondary programs. _____
18. I understand how to apply for grants, scholarships, and other financial awards for which I may be eligible to fund my postsecondary plans. _____
19. I have applied for grants, scholarships, and other financial awards for which I may be eligible to fund my postsecondary plans. _____
20. I have a plan for transition to my life beyond high school. _____

Topic: High School Graduation Requirements

Grade Level: 9
Format: Large group classroom guidance lesson
Goal: Students will become familiar with high school graduation requirements (see ASCA "Mindsets and Behaviors for Student Success," 2014; related standards M3, B-SMS10)
Materials: Exit tickets

Procedure:

1. Introduce high school transition to students. Discuss skills and attitudes needed for successful transition. Emphasize strengths students possess that will contribute to their high school success.
2. Discuss graduation requirements. Use online resources and/or printed materials to aid the discussion on requirements for graduation.
3. Emphasize required credits or course counts in a four-year plan. Discuss electives and optional courses of study.
4. Introduce tests and required assessments. Share typical testing schedule (grade the assessments are taken) and general information about the tests.

Textbox 8.2   Exit Ticket

Name: _____

Period: _____

Date: _____

List two skills or traits that will support your successful transition to high school

How many credits or courses are needed in order to graduate?
- How many credits or courses in English? How many will you have earned at the end of 9th grade?
- How many credits or courses in math? How many will you have earned at the end of 9th grade?
- How many credits in science? How many will you have earned at the end of 9th grade?
- How many credits in social studies? How many will you have earned at the end of 9th grade?
- How many elective credits? How many will you have earned at the end of 9th grade?

What assessments must be passed in order to graduate?

Which ones will you have taken by the end of 9th grade?

5. Discuss other appropriate graduation requirements like community service.
6. Discuss diploma and certificate options.
7. Ask students to identify how many of the discussed requirements they will have met after the successful completion of their ninth grade year.

Assessment: Completion of exit ticket.

Topic: Job Skills / Job Interview

Grade Level: 9–10
Format: Large group classroom guidance lesson
Goal: Students will discuss and practice basic job interview processes (see ASCA "Mindsets and Behaviors for Student Success," 2014; related standards M2, M6, B-SS1, B-SS2, B-SS9 B-LS7 and B-SMS3)
Materials: Student's notebook paper for two-minute reflections
Procedure:

1. Ask students how many of them are planning on getting a job during the summer or during their high school years. Explain to students that now that they are teenagers, many of them will be eligible to secure work permits to work in local businesses, agencies, or organizations. Work permits are needed for students who are under the age of 18 and are an important part of the process for employment for students. Explain how students can secure work permits.
2. Explain to students that the job interview is also an important part of the process as it allows employers to evaluate a possible employee's potential to be successful in a job. Job offers are typically made only after successful interviews.
3. Ask students to brainstorm questions and/or requests that any employer would want to ask or give a first-time employee to make certain the potential employee would be successful. For this activity, help students shape broad questions that would be relevant for many jobs rather than those that focus on particular job specific skills. Questions may include:

   Tell me a little about yourself.
   Why do you want this job?
   What are your strengths?
   What are your weaknesses?
4. Share with students that developing their skill and comfort with answering these types of questions will help them prepare for any first job. Ask

students to work in triads to role-play that they are interviewing for either a babysitting job, pet sitting job, or helping customers behind the counter at a small restaurant or local business. One student should role-play the employer, while another student should role-play the interviewee. The third student should serve as an observer.
5. Allow the students to role-play for about five minutes using the questions that were brainstormed. After the five- to ten-minute role-play, allow the student who was the observer to provide feedback to the interviewee on what was good about the interview and what could be improved. Comments should include reflection on interviewee's listening skills, body language, eye contact, enthusiasm, clarity of expression, positive attitude, and ability to avoid distractions or cause distractions.
6. Repeat the process two more times so that each student has the opportunity to play the interviewee.
7. Bring the class together and ask the students to write a two-minute reflection on one new thing they learned or experienced regarding interviews for jobs.

Assessment: Student completed two-minute reflection.

Topic: Decision Making and Career Planning

Grade Level: 10–11
Format: Small counseling group
Goal: Students will explore the connection between career decision making and effective planning (see ASCA "Mindsets and Behaviors for Student Success," 2014; related standards M4, B-LS1, B-LS4, B-LS7, B-LS9, B-SS1, B-SS2, B-SS3)
Materials: Chairs for small group counseling setting
Procedure:

1. Ask students to imagine that they are going on a trip and they can only take five items with them. Ask them to think about and list the items they would pack, assuming that their food and shelter needs would be provided. Allow students about five minutes for this activity.
2. Encourage group members to share their lists with a partner in the group. Invite students to think about the ways their lists are similar to and different from their partner's list.
3. Discuss with students that they made decisions about what would be on their list of five items. Talk about the factors that influenced their deci-

sions. These may include perceived practicality, perceived utility, habits, likes, and values.
4. Explain that the students were not given much detail about the trip. Ask them how their lists would have changed if they knew more details about the trip, like the location, what they would do while on the trip, and how long the trip would last. Allow students to come to the understanding that the more they knew about where they were going, the better they would have been able to prepare for the trip.
5. Highlight similarities between this exercise and career and college planning. Talk with students about the importance of having good, reliable information, good decision-making processes, and clear goals about where they are headed.
6. Using a go-around, invite students to share where they are headed in their postsecondary plans. As students share, ask each group member to offer one question that will help the other group members clarify and learn more about where they are headed. These questions do not have to be answered immediately in the session, but should serve as points of consideration for the group members. For example, one group member may say, "After high school I am planning to be a music executive." Questions offered by the other group members to help sharpen the plans could be:

"What does a music executive do?"
"Where does a music executive work?"
"Are there many jobs available?"
"What skills does a music executive need?"
"Does a music executive have to be a musician?"
"What kind of training do you need to be a music executive?"
"Do you have to go to college to be a music executive?"

7. At the end of group session, ask each member to select one question they were asked about where they are headed and come to the next group session prepared to answer the question. Explain that students may need to do research, talk with their peers, teachers, or mentors, or contact an expert to get the answer for themselves. Ask students to share the one question related to their career path they will explore in a quick go-around.
8. Close the group session by summarizing the activity and the connection of adequate preparation to clear knowledge of where one is headed for postsecondary plans.

Assessment: Identified career question.

Topic: Resume

Grade Level: 9–10
Format: Classroom guidance lesson
Goal: Students will complete a resume (see ASCA "Mindsets and Behaviors for Student Success," 2014; related standards M2, M5, B-LS7, B-SMS3, B-SS1, B-SS8)
Materials: Resume Template, computer access for each student
Procedure:

1. Introduce the topic of resumes and ask students why they are useful. Explain that resumes change over time as individuals gain more experiences.
2. Share the Resume Template and explain the purpose of each part. Explain that students can choose to replace the "career objective" section with a "summary" section that includes two or three brief sentences that explain their professional strengths and skills. Both the career objective section and the summary section must be carefully worded to let potential employers know your intentions and a little about who you are as a potential employee.
3. Discuss the importance of using verbs in the resume (i.e., led, coordinated, produced, planned, played, wrote). Explain how these words help potential employers understand the skills you have demonstrated in past activities and experiences.
4. Give students one class period to prepare the first draft of their resume. Encourage students to select the most important experiences, activities, and awards so that they can keep their resumes to one page in length.
5. Encourage students to proofread carefully and to make sure they use a consistent, easily readable font.
6. Collect resumes and provide students with individualized feedback. Return and review resumes during individual advising sessions.

Assessment: Completed student resumes.

Resume Template
Name
Address
Phone Number
Email

Career Objective
(Sample) To use my _____, _____, and _____ skills to provide excellent babysitting services to neighborhood children.
Education/School, class of 20XX, GPA

Experience and Location
- Bullet list of work or volunteer experiences and the location. Start each bullet with an action verb.

Activities
- Bullet list of extracurricular activities. Include years of participation.

Awards
- Bullet list of awards. Include year awarded.

References
"Available upon request" or provide a bullet list of three names and their contact information. These names should not be names of immediate family members or other relatives.

Topic: Financial Aid

Grade Level: 10–11
Format: Classroom guidance lesson
Goal: Students will understand the basic types of financial aid and ways to begin a financial aid search (see ASCA "Mindsets and Behaviors for Student Success," 2014; related standards M2, M4, B-LS7, B-SMS1, B-SMS7, B-SMS10, B-SS8)
Materials: Classroom guidance setting, internet access, and projector for YouTube clips
Procedure:

1. Introduce the topic of financial aid for postsecondary educational expenses including college and career school. Discuss the four basic types of financial aid and their differences:

   - Scholarships—typically awarded based on academic performance, skills, or special talents. May be awarded by a particular institution, or private agency, or the state. Scholarships typically do not need to be repaid.
   - Grants—typically awarded based on need. Typically do not need to be paid back. The Pell Grant is an example of this type of financial aid.
   - Loans—May or may not be based on need. Must be repaid. Loans may be offered by federal or private source.
   - Work-study—Need-based financial aid. Students are offered part-time jobs, typically on the college campus or location affiliated with the campus, that help pay for college costs.

2. Explain that students must initially demonstrate and continue to demonstrate eligibility for financial aid for the entire time that they receive the

aid. Explain the eligibility requirements for federal financial aid include educational requirements, acceptance, and/or enrollment requirements, citizenship or eligible noncitizen status, having a social security number, and selective service registration for men.

3. Explain that students who are not citizens may be eligible for some merit scholarships, state scholarships, college awards, or in some cases, in-state tuition rates. Explain that undocumented students are not eligible for federal financial aid; however, there may be aid available. Encourage all students to not give up when it comes to searching for aid sources for which they are eligible. Stress the importance of thorough searches for scholarships and awards. Talk about the ways small award amounts can add up to significantly help students meet their financial needs.

4. Show video overview of the financial aid process. This 1:47 minute YouTube clip reviews the basic types of financial aid and the role of the federal financial aid office, https://www.youtube.com/watch?v=kbJ55UWMEFE.

5. Watch video clip highlighting types of federal financial aid. This 2.14 minute YouTube clip provides more detail about the types of federal financial aid, https://www.youtube.com/watch?annotation_id=annotation_2419155109&feature=iv&list=PL5164CE4355C66FCB&src_vid=H_iS7gmQd9o&v=Pn4OECMTh5w.

6. Emphasize that the Free Application for Federal Student Aid (FAFSA) is the form most students will complete to be considered for financial aid. The FASFA is used to determine eligibility for financial aid and requires detailed information about a family's finances. Explain that the new form for the upcoming academic year becomes available in October, but families must wait until after January 1 to submit it. Explain that families should submit the FAFSA as soon after January 1 as possible since there are priority deadlines that help students receive the best consideration for available financial aid dollars.

7. Ask for questions based on the videos or the information discussed. Explain that it is never too early to think and talk about ways to pay for postsecondary education. Emphasize that students should not assume they cannot afford college or a career school. Explain that the search for scholarship and aid dollars that match each individual student's needs takes time and persistence. Students can begin free scholarship searches through the office of Federal Student Aid (https://studentaid.ed.gov/sa/types/grants-scholarships/finding-scholarships#how-find), library resources, community organizations, local businesses, and the school counselors' office.

8. Remind students that financial aid scams do exist. Advise them to always talk with the school counselor, an admissions counselor, or other trusted

adults before they pursue, pay for, or sign any agreement regarding aid or help securing aid.
9. Ask students to make an appointment with the school counselor to discuss their individual needs and begin to explore resources that will help them meet their postsecondary plans.
10. As a summary for the lesson, ask students to identify the four major sources of financial aid, the sources that typically do not have to be repaid, the form used to apply for federal financial aid, when that form should be submitted, and at least two ways to begin the search for financial resources for college and career schools.

Assessment: Students' oral responses to summary questions.

Topic: Choosing a College

Grade Level: 10
Format: Classroom guidance lesson
Goal: Students will identify key areas to consider when choosing a college (see ASCA "Mindsets and Behaviors for Student Success," 2014; related standards M4, B-LS1, B-LS7, B-SMS3, B-SS1)
Materials: Classroom guidance setting, chart paper or white board, notebook paper, pencils or pens
Procedure:

1. Introduce the topic of college choice and ask students how many of them have started to think about if they want to attend college and where they may want to attend.
2. Explain that it is okay if students have not made up their minds. Explain that whether to attend college and when to attend college are important decisions that they will make in the next year or so. Remind students that the most important thing is to remain open to all possible options.
3. Let students brainstorm important things they think should be considered when deciding which college to attend. As students offer points to consider, chart their responses. Lead discussions on why each listed item is important to consider when choosing a college.
4. Be sure the charted list includes a consideration of the students' strengths, abilities, weaknesses, or needs; the kind of college (i.e., two year, four year, residential, commuter); the size of the college (big, small, medium); the location of the college (within state, close by, far away); programs, fields of study, or distinctive areas; cocurricular activities; admission requirements (including application, GPA, test scores, interviews, recommendations, and essays); and costs.

5. Emphasize that while costs are important, colleges should not be ruled out because of assumed costs. Explain that many students are eligible for financial aid that make colleges more affordable.
6. Explain that all these factors work together to help students determine a college that may best fit their needs. Explain that just because a college may be a perfect fit for one student does not mean it will be a perfect choice for another.
7. Invite students to reflect on the items listed in item 4 and any additional items they brainstormed. Ask them to write a paragraph about their preferences for college as they understand them at this early point in their college exploration. Their paragraph should address each item or area on the charted list. Let the students know that is okay if they are not sure what they want at this point. Explain that this is just one of many chances they will get to think about and write about their emerging college preferences.
8. Ask students to share their drafts with a partner. Allow partners to ask questions of each other regarding their emerging thoughts about college choice. Invite three or four students to share their drafts with the entire class.
9. Encourage students to use resources including online resources, printed materials in the school counselors' office or college counselors' office, and school counselor meetings to begin to identify colleges that align with their preferences expressed in their paragraphs. Give students a reasonable timeline to begin this research independently (perhaps one to two weeks).
10. As a summary to this lesson, ask students to list four items that should be considered when choosing a college. Ask students to verbally state why each listed item is important to the college choice.

Assessment: Paragraph on choosing a college and follow-up on identifying specific colleges that meet the individual student's criteria.

Topic: Common Application and the College Essay

Grade Level: 11
Format: Classroom guidance lesson
Goal: Students will complete a first draft of their college essay (see ASCA "Mindsets and Behaviors for Student Success," 2014; related standards M1, M2, M4, M5, B-LS1, B-LS2, B-LS3, B-LS4, B-LS5 B-LS8, B-SMS1, B-SMS3,B-SS1)
Materials: Classroom guidance setting, internet access, and projector for YouTube clips

Procedure:

1. Introduce students to the Common Application. Explain that the application is accepted by more than 750 colleges and universities and requires general information that is consistently required by colleges and universities like students' grades, transcripts, test scores, listing of extracurricular activities, and parent information.
2. Explain while many students who plan to go to college will complete the Common Application, some may have to complete additional documents for their chosen schools. Others may have to complete entirely separate applications because their chosen college or university does not accept the Common Application at all.
3. Explain that almost all applications require a college essay. Explain the role that essays have on college applications.
4. Be sure to let students know that the essay is an opportunity for college admission officers to get to know who they are beyond their test scores, grades, and accomplishments. Explain that the essay is an important component of the college application process that allows the students' personality to shine.
5. Explain that while the essay prompts may vary, most will be broad. Explain that the Common Application typically has broad essay questions. Share some sample essay prompts using the Common Application website: http://www.commonapp.org/whats-appening/application-updates/2018-2019-common-application-essay-prompts.
6. In collaboration with an English teacher or team, allow students to select one of the prompts from the Common Application or other college essay prompt to develop a first draft. Limit the draft to 650 words.
7. Set a reasonable due date for the first draft. Remind students that the draft will be revised multiple times before they submit it as part of their application for college.

Assessment: First draft of a college essay.

Topic: Stress Management

Grade Level: 9–12
Format: Small counseling group
Goal: Students will discuss stress and identify and practice healthy techniques for managing it (see ASCA "Mindsets and Behaviors for Student Success," 2014; related standards M1, M6, B-SMS1, B-SMS2, B-SMS7, B-SMS8, B-SMS10, B-SS1, B-SS2, B-SS6, B-SS8, B-SS9)

Materials: Chairs for small group counseling setting
Procedure:

1. Open the group counseling session by introducing the topic of stress. Explain that we all experience stress from time to time. Explain that too much stress can be unhealthy.
2. Invite students to share stressors high school students may experience. These could include homework, tests, friends or relationship concerns, bullies or bullying behavior, social media, parents or home situations, college pressure, or fear and uncertainty about life after high school.
3. Ask students to identify their own personal signs that the stress they are experiencing is reaching an unhealthy level. If the group has not reached a full working stage of development, this reflection may not be appropriate. In those cases ask students to reflect on general (not personal) signs of too much stress.
4. Discuss healthy and nonhealthy ways to manage stress. Ask students to identify healthy ways they have managed their stress related to the issues above. Ways could include deep breathing, exercise, time management/ planning, guided imagery, and progressive muscle relaxation.
5. Lead students in a deep breathing exercise. Invite students to quiet and center themselves. When settled, ask them to put one hand on their chest and one on their belly. Encourage them to breathe in deeply and slowly, perhaps to a count of four, ensuring that their diaphragm expands. Hold their breath for a brief count, and exhale slowly through their mouth, perhaps to a count of four. Ask them to repeat this breathing pattern four to six times.
6. Encourage students to share how they felt during and after the deep breathing exercise. If they found the deep breathing to be relaxing, ask them when they could use the strategy.
7. Lead students in a guided imagery exercise. Invite students to quiet and center themselves. When settled, invite them to breathe deeply one or two times and close their eyes. Ask them to picture a calm, peaceful place they enjoy. Ask the students to imagine themselves in the place. Invite them to add as much detail to their image as they can. Silently, let students see themselves in their desired peaceful settings for two to three minutes.
8. Using a calm voice, tell students they must prepare to leave their settings. Ask students to open their eyes and rejoin the group when they are ready.
9. Encourage students to share how they felt during and after the guided imagery exercise. If they found the guided imagery exercise to be relaxing, ask them when they could use the strategy to manage their stress.

10. In closing, ask students to share what they learned or affirmed about themselves during the session. Ask them to identify one healthy stress management technique they will commit to trying before the next group session.

Assessment: Closing go-around related to intrapersonal learning and commitment to use a healthy stress management technique.

Topic: Transitions

Grade Level: 11–12
Format: Small counseling group
Goal: Students will discuss the transition from high school and identify supports and plans for a successful transition (see ASCA "Mindsets and Behaviors for Student Success," 2014; related standards M1, M2, M5, B-LS9, B-SMS1, B-SMS7, B-SMS10, B-SS1, B-SS2, B-SS3, B-SS4)
Materials: Chairs for small group counseling setting, index cards, and pens or pencils
Procedure:

1. Open the group counseling session by introducing the topic of transition. Ask the students to identify the transitions they have made recently. These may include transition to a new class, transition to a new community, and transition to high school.
2. Ask the group members to consider the transition they are about to make to life beyond high school. Allow students to write down challenges or concerns they may have about the transition on index cards. Students should not write their names on the cards. Ask students to place the index cards face down in a pile in the center of the group. The school counselor may make a few of these challenge or concern cards ahead of time to add to the pile. Challenges or concerns could include: "I do not know what I want to do after high school graduation," "I did not get into my first choice college and I am upset," "I do not have enough money to get the tech certification I want," "I do not want to leave my friends," "I am scared about everything."
3. Allow student volunteers to select a card from the pile and read the challenge or concern to the group.
4. Engage the group in a discussion to clarify the challenge or concern and ways to approach it. Focus the discussion on supports that may be available to help students facing the selected challenge or concern.
5. Allow the group to work through three to five additional cards, as time allows.

6. As a summary and closing, ask students to share what they learned during the session that may be most helpful to them as they think about their individual transition from high school. Ask students what supports or plans may prove helpful. Use a go-around to hear from each student.

Assessment: Go-around summary activity.

Topic: Career Awareness

Grade Level: 9–10
Format: Large group classroom guidance lesson
Goal: Students will identify career clusters of interest (see ASCA "Mindsets and Behaviors for Student Success," 2014; related standards M4, B-LS1, B-LS5, B-LS7, B-SMS3, BSS1)
Materials: Computers with internet access (perhaps within the school media center)
Procedure:

1. Remind students of their previous work exploring career clusters. Remind students that jobs fall into one of 16 career clusters. Discuss that many of them will not hold the same job throughout their work careers. Explain that they may, however, hold several jobs during their 30–40 years of work that fall in the same career cluster or call on their skills and interests in different ways.
2. Allow students to work independently to complete the Career Awareness worksheet using information from the following websites: Bureau of Labor Statistics, Career Outlook, https://www.bls.gov/careeroutlook/2015/article/career-clusters.htm# and Occupational Outlook Handbook: https://www.bls.gov/ooh/.
3. Collect the worksheet and include a copy or summary of the information in students' independent learning plans.

Assessment: Student completion of the Career Awareness worksheet.

Career Awareness Worksheet

Name   Date: Class:

1. Identify two career clusters that interest you. List two job titles in the selected cluster that interest you?

Cluster 1:	Cluster 2:
Job title-	Job title-
Job title-	Job title-

2. List 3 high school courses that you might take to help prepare you for a job in that cluster.

Cluster 1:	Cluster 2:
• High school course-	• High school course-
• High school course-	• High school course-
• High school course-	• High school course-

3. List an extra-curricular activity that may help you prepare for a job in each of your selected clusters.

Cluster 1:	Cluster 2:
• Extra-curricular activity	• Extra-curricular activity

4. Complete the following chart for each job title listed in number 1 above:

Job Title	College Degree Required?	Median Income	Anticipated Job Outlook

Figure 8.1.

Topic: Social Skills

Grade Level: 11–12

Format: Large group classroom guidance lesson

Goal: Students will demonstrate noncognitive work skills (see ASCA "Mindsets and Behaviors for Student Success," 2014; related standards M2, M5, M6, B-LS1, B-LS2, B-SMS1, B-SMS2, B-SMS3, B-SMS7, B-SS1, B-SS2, B-SS6, B-SS7, and B-SS9)

Materials: Ninth Grade Program Idea worksheet for each student

Procedure:

1. Ask students to think back to their ninth grade year of high school. Ask them to think about the needs of ninth graders and reflect on the programs and activities that helped them the most during that year. Ask them to think about the programs and activities that they did not have that could have helped them had they been in place.
2. Challenge the students to work in groups of three to four to design a ninth grade program or activity that meets a specific need of ninth graders. Let the students know their group must determine a need and goals to meet the need, design an approach or activity, and determine how they will know the activity or approach has been successful. Tell students they have $1,000 to spend on this event, and that the group must come to consensus about the activity and the way to spend the money.
3. Allow students to work in groups for 25 minutes to complete the activity. Ask students to complete the first box on the worksheet according to their group's plans.
4. Have each team briefly share their ideas with the entire class.
5. Ask the students how they worked together as a team. Ask them what behaviors they used when working as a team to complete the given task. Have them identify what helped them work together well. Students may say things like, we listened, showed respect, collaborated, adapted, showed kindness, were creative, set goals (noncognitive work skills). List the skills as the students share them.
6. Explain to the students that these same skills will help them as they enter the world of work. Talk about the important role of teams in the workplace. Explain that some employers identify these essential skills as noncognitive work skills.
7. Read aloud the student generated list of noncognitive work skills.
8. To close the lesson, ask the students to complete a paragraph reflection on the noncognitive skills they used or should have used as their team worked and how those skills could help them in the world of work.

9. To expand this lesson, students could be encouraged to share the strongest program ideas with the student government association, class president, or parent group.

Assessment: Students' reflection on their noncognitive work skills and ways they may contribute to work success.

Textbox 8.3   Ninth Grade Program Idea

Name: _____ Date: _____

Need/Problem/Issue:

Program/Activity Overview:

Program/Activity Goals:

Budget:

Textbox 8.4   Reflection

Essential Non-Cognitive Skills:

Contributions to Work Place Success:

ACTIVITIES AND IDEAS

Open Access Web-based Programs—Explore open access web-based programs or websites for information and developmentally appropriate activities related to college and career readiness. These resources may be provided by the U.S. Department of Labor, private businesses or industries, or professional organizations or affiliated bodies committed to college and career readiness.

Collages—Work with students in a small counseling group setting to complete collages that show who they are. These collages will help students begin to better understand their interests and skills. These collages can be used as discussion starters for conversations regarding identifying career goals.

College Day—To increase college awareness and create excitement around college attendance, invite students and teachers to dress in college apparel or their favorite college colors. Update college resources in the school counseling office. Prepare special displays or bulletin boards with teachers' and recent graduates' colleges. As seniors make their college decisions, add these school logos to the displays. This information can be displayed in charts or through displays that include college mascots or logos.

College Visits—Partner with local community groups or nonprofit organizations to support or advertise short college visits and extended, overnight college visits. Many sororities, fraternities, and local community groups with educational missions sponsor college bus tours for high school students. Work with the school administration and/or local colleges' admissions office to support transportation for students for short, single day or partial day tours. Arrange for students to actually sit in on classes during their college tours, whenever possible.

College Fair—Partner with other district high schools or community organizations to sponsor a college fair. Encourage students to attend the fair with a list of specific questions to answer a specific number of colleges. Questions can include what is the college's name, location, distinctive programs, costs, strengths, and weaknesses. Students' notes can be turned in for extra credit or can be material for individual learning plans.

College Goal Sunday Programs—Advertise any College Goal Sunday programs or other Free Application for Federal Student Aid (FAFSA) completion programs in your area. If no events are planned in your immediate area, partner with other high school counselors to provide times when families can access technology and receive appropriate support to complete the FAFSA.

Tests—Hold information sessions for students and families regarding common standardized tests used in the college admission process. Include information regarding test structure and overview, dates, fees and fee waiver policies, registration processes, free test preparation resources, score ranges, and testing site locations. Prepare and distribute information packets in multiple languages as needed by your community.

First Job Opportunities—Invite local employers who have a strong record of offering teens volunteer experiences and job opportunities to come to a workshop for students. Encourage the employers to talk with students about the skills, behaviors, attitudes, and steps necessary for students to be successful in their first job or volunteer work experience. Hands-on components of the workshop could include introduction to work permits, work applications, and interview processes.

Speaker Series—Invite recent alumni to come back to high school to talk with small groups of students about their experiences in the world of work and college. Select a diverse group of speakers to talk with students and answer their informal questions regarding transition, college, and career.

Postsecondary Preparation Programs—Invite faculty and students from community postsecondary training programs to talk with students in a career fair format. Encourage the faculty and their students to bring hands-on activities, displays, and handouts in addition to preparing to talk with the students and answering their questions. Community-based postsecondary preparation programs, including ones for cosmetology, truck driving, nurse's aide, and technology certification, offer students exposure to a wide array of important career options.

Financial Aid Workshop—Invite students and their families to an evening or weekend program that overviews general college costs and considerations. Include specific resources regarding federal, state, and local aid programs. Invite a local university financial aid officer or local experts to present and answer student and family questions. Make school resources and supports available for families to gather additional information or complete applications for local scholarships and complete online Free Application for Federal Student Aid (FASFA) forms. Provide a resource packet and serve dinner to workshop attendees.

Loan and Money Management Workshop—Invite students and their families to an evening or weekend workshop that discusses student loans, default issues, and key principles of money management for college-aged students. Select reputable community experts to present or lead question and answer sessions. This session could be part of a larger financial aid workshop or a separate workshop that focuses on students' and families' questions about loans and general financial planning.

Success Mentors—Pair selected ninth graders with selected tenth grade success mentors. Mentors and mentees should meet at least one time every other week during the first marking period to help the new ninth grade mentees manage the transition to high school. The experience will help the ninth and tenth grade students gain and strengthen noncognitive skills (e.g., social skills, cooperation, focus, persistence, organizational skills, commitment) that are necessary for success in career and college. The success mentees and their mentors can celebrate at the end of the first marking period with a brief awards ceremony and pizza party.

Chapter Nine

What Is Next?

This chapter discusses future needs and directions of college and career readiness counseling for K–12 school counselors. Special attention is given to emerging technologies, policy, and educational trends.

NEXT STEPS

The need for America's youth to enter the global economy college and career ready is unquestionable. As students graduate from high school they must have the knowledge and skills necessary to immediately and successfully enter the workforce or college. The world of today and tomorrow demands the active participation of all citizens. We cannot afford to have any of our youth sit out or be cast aside. In a very real sense, this demands that every student succeed.

While schools and school counselors have for decades been committed to the work of college and career readiness for students, our new global context demands new approaches. This book has outlined a developmental approach that suggests the work of college and career readiness begins not in secondary schools, but in elementary schools. College and career readiness is a proposition that starts with our youngest students as they begin to develop career awareness and a sense of self. College choice begins not as an eleventh or twelfth grade task or checklist, but as engaging student-centered learning activities and exploration in elementary school.

The thread of developmental college and career readiness offers a bright future for students and the school counselors who are privileged to work with them. Future career and college readiness work must continue to evolve and consider new approaches. The details of these new approaches are hard to predict. What appears clear, however, is that career and college readiness work of the future must focus on areas of cultural competence and advocacy, technology, and evaluation.

Cultural Competence and Advocacy

As discussed in a previous chapter in this book, school counselors play a critical role in ensuring access and equity for our diverse student population. School counselors hold significant social capital for students, thus providing access to information, networks, norms, and support. Social capital is a key in effective college and career readiness pathways. This may be even truer in the years to come.

The nation today and tomorrow cannot fulfill the dreams of its founders without a productive citizenry. Today, this citizenry is diverse. As time moves on, this citizenry will only continue to grow more richly diverse. In 2014 the nation's public schools enrolled more students of color than White students. The National Center for Educational Statistics (Hussar & Bailey, 2017) projections show a continuation of this trend for the next several years. While these data capture trends regarding student population, race, ethnicity, gender, and some measures of socioeconomic status, they do not capture the full scope of student diversity that includes gender identity, sexual orientation, religion, and the full range of student ability among many other factors.

Given these projections and trends, cultural competence will move from a tangential skill set to an essential core competency for school counselors. Cultural competence is an ethical responsibility for school counselors and a mandate for effective school counseling. Cultural competence is an important ideal in school counseling, yet its centrality in career and college readiness counseling has significant practical implications.

Current data report low unemployment rates, yet may fields report the inability to find enough skilled workers to fill job vacancies. This trend may only continue or worsen in future years. Young people, therefore, must be prepared not just with college and career readiness approaches, but with college and career readiness approaches that are developed and implemented by school counselors who have significant expertise in the skills, knowledge, attitudes, and beliefs of counseling that is culturally competent.

This national need for employees demands that no individuals can be lost or overlooked. Every individual of our increasingly diverse community holds potential for continued American success. Counselors must work with students in culturally relevant ways, but they must also have a level of expertise that allows them to share these important skills with students so that students' interactions are culturally inclusive.

Whether students are working on competencies related to collaboration, leadership, or developing positive and supportive relationships—all of which are significantly tied to career and college readiness skills—students must increasingly demonstrate these skills in culturally competent ways. ASCA's "Mindsets and Behaviors for Student Success" (2014) prioritize student skills in effective work with diverse others. This must continue.

Additionally, school counselors must advocate for students and families in ways that move beyond the local schoolhouse. While school level advocacy is important, the work of college and career readiness of the future will require an informed and sophisticated look at systems and national policy in ways aimed at eradicating prejudice, bias, discrimination, and oppression as it manifests in ways that suppress the ability of young people, all young people, to become college and career ready.

This work may take school counselors out of their comfort zones as they, through individual acts and collective, professional organizational work, take active positions on issues such as immigration, social media use, gun control, marijuana legalization, climate change, environmental pollution, poverty, and juvenile detention just to name a few. The voice of the school counselor is important and must be heard as we wrestle with these issues nationally.

School counselor advocacy can and must take on various forms. Working toward the aim of college and career readiness for all students, for example, a school counselor could work as a community change agent to address environmental pollution issues that keep a significant portion of his school district student population out of school due to asthma-related health concerns. Or, serving as another example, a school counselor committed to college and career readiness for all students could commit to raising public awareness about immigration policies and implications for students in her community. She could take this further as an advocate and serve as a liaison between stakeholders in significant immigration conversations throughout her state.

Future school counselors must be ever ready and prepared to take on the role of advocacy in pursuit of ensuring college and career readiness for all students. Counselors' preparedness to take on these roles must be grounded in rich professional development such as workshop attendance and continuing education opportunities, advanced coursework, and strong clinical supervision.

Technology

Technology is widely used in career and college planning. Some school counselors currently use open access, web-based programs for students' career exploration. Some school systems have invested in comprehensive college and career readiness platforms that are used throughout the school district, while some school counselors frequently access college websites in classroom guidance or individual student planning sessions.

In some cases, forms students use for employment or college applications are accessed and submitted exclusively using electronic tools. Also, comprehensive tools for individual learning plans are often offered through online platforms. School counselors and teachers alike may use technology for virtual tours, learning games, and content related quizzes or surveys. For years, school counselors effectively have helped students gain access to these resources across the expanse of the digital divide that still negatively and disproportionately affects some student populations.

In the years to come, school counselors will continue to use technology in these ways. There may, however, need to be consideration of using technology in broader ways to help students meet career and college readiness competencies.

For example, many school counselors already use emails and texts to reach out to students with information about upcoming college and career events and deadlines. Imagine a broader integration of technology. Imagine the widespread use of online meeting platforms to bring together families for information sessions about financial aid basics and general transition information and deadlines. This use has the potential to make college and career readiness information more readily available to families who reside in a variety of geographic locations and those for whom physically meeting is an extreme challenge.

Digital pedagogies also offer great opportunities for students to meet educational goals. This may be particularly true for students in rural communities or students whose emotional, medical, or physical needs make attending a traditional brick and mortar school unsustainable. As more K–12 schools offer online options, school counselors must consider how career and college programs should be delivered using these platforms. While the broader counseling profession has begun to explore the practical and ethical implications of counseling using technology, this may be new territory for most school counselors.

Of course, each delivery mode as it relates to career and college readiness counseling should be considered for its suitability for delivery in online contexts. What are the strengths and limitations of individual counseling for students' career and college counseling online? Can classroom guidance career and college readiness lessons authentically be translated to online platforms? If so, how? Does group counseling have a meaningful and effective application in the online environment? What are the ethical implications for technology use in counseling? What are the specific ethical implications of using technology and online intervention modes with students who are minors?

These questions and many others face school counselors as they consider the future of career and college readiness programs for K–12 students. The future use of technology in college and career readiness school counseling work, like the future application of cultural competence and advocacy skills, requires school counselors' continued commitment to counselor professional development, advanced coursework, and clinical supervision.

Evaluation

Schools and school systems are adopting rigorous curricula to make sure students have the requisite skills in core content areas. These state and district level plans and efforts for reform often are tailored to specifically meet the needs of students in the community with an eye on future global needs and trends.

In the best cases, school counselors are a part of these discussions as they work to help students meet career and college readiness goals. In these best case situations, there is a strong recognition that rigorous academic curricula and plans for school reform offer important opportunities for the intersection of that curriculum work and college and career readiness goals.

The importance of this work for the successful future of our students demands that we use evidence-based approaches. No longer can we rely on simply doing what has been done in the past or whatever is the current educational trend or innovation. Limited resources, limited time, and most importantly, the vast needs of our students and our nation demand a laser focus on curricular and pedagogical approaches that work.

Some school counselors are conducting small-scale evaluations to measure the effectiveness and value of their programs on a routine basis. The evaluations provide important data on student outcomes, perceptions, and areas of needed growth. These data can also provide insight on necessary programmatic changes and counselor performance.

As we consider future trends for the field, however, a final consideration must be related to these practices and approaches. School counselors should increase and strengthen partnerships with counselor educators and other researchers to commit to quality small, localized action research projects and, importantly, rich, large-scale studies. In particular, rigorous large scale studies may provide the much needed data to promote the understanding and use of evidence-based practices in school counseling career and college readiness programs across various student populations and contexts.

Goals, objectives, strategies, indicators, and benchmarks for K–12 provide opportunities for evaluation and may suggest future avenues for student growth regarding career and college readiness. The partnership between researcher and practitioner that emerges when school counselors take on this work with research colleagues adds an important, unique voice and perspective to the work. The issues of implementation and accessibility to the research are more likely to be addressed when these partnerships are in place. The partnership embraces the realities of work in school settings with the benefit of a skilled, counseling professional with first-hand knowledge that witnesses the effects the work has on the lives of students, their families, and school communities.

Career and college readiness approaches must be advanced through rigorous, research-based evaluation. The results of more rigorous evaluation will substantively enhance school counseling and may lead to more positive outcomes for students' potential across large populations in diverse settings.

As assessment considerations align with state and school level curricula, school counselors must advocate the inclusion of career and college readiness competencies. This wide discussion and consideration of career and college readiness competencies will help to make certain there is wide acceptance of these important goals.

The data, however, must suggest effectiveness for continued use of programs and approaches. Data are important for the future of the entire counseling field. The area of college and career readiness, however, absolutely demands this level of rigor. The future of our students, the future of our nation, and in no small part the future of our global societies demand it.

Appendix
College and Career Planning Calendar

ELEMENTARY SCHOOL

This calendar includes many major items for a K–12 college and career readiness program. This calendar can be used by school counselors as part of their planning for a comprehensive college and career readiness school counseling program.

September

- Review college and career readiness goals and competencies for the K–5 program. Share plan with administrators, teachers, families, and other appropriate partners.
- Begin college and career awareness classroom guidance program.
- Plan activities for National Career Development Month.
- Introduce college and career readiness goals, competencies, and curriculum to families at Back to School Night.

October

- Continue college and career readiness classroom guidance program.
- Begin small group counseling program related to college and career awareness.
- Plan activities for National Career Development Month.

November

- Celebrate National Career Development Month [National Career Development Association (NCDA)].

- Continue classroom and small group counseling program related to career awareness.

December

- Continue classroom and small group counseling program related to career awareness.

January

- Revisit college and career readiness goals and conduct a midyear assessment.
- Begin transition planning for fifth grade students.
- Continue classroom and small group counseling program related to career awareness.
- Plan schoolwide career awareness event.
- Make plans for National School Counselor Week.

February

- Celebrate National School Counselor Week.
- Continue transition planning for fifth grade students. Plan information/planning meetings with families, as necessary.
- Plan schoolwide career awareness event.
- Continue classroom and small group counseling program related to career awareness.

March

- Continue classroom and small group counseling program related to career awareness.
- Implement schoolwide career awareness event.

April

- Continue classroom and small group counseling program related to career awareness.

May

- Conclude classroom and small group counseling program related to career awareness for the year.

June

- Evaluate current college and career readiness program.
- Review and share data and outcomes with all stakeholders.
- Set college and career readiness goals for following academic year.

MIDDLE SCHOOL

September

- Review college and career readiness goals and competencies for 6–8 program. Share plan with administrators, teachers, families, and other appropriate partners.
- Begin college and career awareness classroom guidance program.
- Plan activities for National Career Development Month.
- Introduce college and career readiness goals, competencies, and curriculum to families at Back to School Night.

October

- Continue college and career readiness classroom guidance program.
- Begin small group counseling program related to college and career awareness.
- Plan activities for National Career Development Month.

November

- Celebrate National Career Development Month [National Career Development Association (NCDA)]
- Continue classroom and small group counseling program related to career awareness.

December

- Continue classroom and small group counseling program related to career awareness.

January

- Revisit college and career readiness goals and conduct a midyear assessment.
- Begin transition planning for eighth grade students. Start students' individual learning plans. Plan information and planning meetings with families.

- Continue classroom and small group counseling program related to career awareness and skills.
- Plan grade level college and career readiness events.
- Make plans for National School Counselor Week.

February

- Celebrate National School Counselor Week.
- Continue transition planning for eighth grade students.
- Plan grade level college and career readiness events.
- Continue classroom and small group counseling program related to career awareness and skills.

March

- Continue classroom and small group counseling program related to career awareness and skills.
- Implement grade level college and career readiness events.

April

- Continue classroom and small group counseling program related to career awareness and skills.
- Hold a Paying for College workshop for interested families.

May

- Conclude classroom and small group counseling program related to career awareness and skills for the year.

June

- Evaluate current college and career readiness program.
- Review and share data and outcomes with all stakeholders.
- Set college and career readiness goals for following academic year.

HIGH SCHOOL

September

- Review college and career readiness goals and competencies for grades 9–12. Share plan with administrators, teachers, families, and other appropriate partners.

- Begin college and career awareness classroom guidance program.
- Plan activities for National Career Development Month.
- Introduce college and career readiness goals, competencies, and curriculum to schoolwide community through newsletter or counselor notice.
- Begin test-taking skills small group or classroom guidance sessions. Publicize important dates and registration details for college entrance tests.
- Review students' individual learning plans. Revise and further develop as necessary.
- Attend or organize college and career fairs, activities, or special sessions.

October

- Continue college and career readiness classroom guidance program.
- Begin individual planning meetings with all students. Take notes to use for letters of recommendation. Include awards, extracurricular activities, volunteer work, and special strengths.
- Begin small group counseling program related to college and career awareness.
- Plan activities for National Career Development Month.
- Review students' individual learning plans. Revise and further develop as necessary.
- Continue test-taking skills small group or classroom guidance sessions. Publicize important dates and registration details for college entrance tests. Outreach as appropriate for tenth, eleventh, and twelfth grade students.
- Attend or organize college and career fairs, activities, or special sessions.
- Plan grade level college and career readiness events, including FAFSA information sessions or completion events.

November

- Celebrate National Career Development Month [National Career Development Association (NCDA)].
- Continue classroom and small group counseling program related to career awareness.
- Continue individual planning meetings with all students. Take notes for letters of recommendation. Include awards, extracurricular activities, volunteer work, and special strengths.
- Attend or organize college and career fairs, activities, or special sessions.
- Continue test-taking skills small group or classroom guidance sessions. Publicize important dates and registration details for college entrance tests. Outreach as appropriate for tenth, eleventh, and twelfth grade students.
- Hold test information and interpretation sessions for students and families.

- Plan grade level college and career readiness events, including FAFSA information sessions or completion events.

December

- Continue classroom and small group counseling program related to career awareness.
- Continue individual planning meetings with all students. Take notes for future letters of recommendation. Include awards, extracurricular activities, volunteer work, and special strengths.
- Hold test information and interpretation sessions for families.
- Continue test-taking skills small group or classroom guidance sessions. Publicize important dates and registration details for college entrance tests. Outreach as appropriate for tenth, eleventh, and twelfth grade students.
- Plan grade level college and career readiness events, including FAFSA information sessions or completion events.

January

- Revisit college and career readiness goals and conduct a midyear assessment.
- Begin transition planning for all students. Plan information and planning meetings with families as appropriate.
- Continue classroom and small group counseling program related to career awareness and skills.
- Continue individual planning meetings with all students. Take notes for future letters of recommendation. Include awards, extracurricular activities, volunteer work, and special strengths.
- Plan grade level college and career readiness events, including FAFSA information sessions or completion events.
- Continue test-taking skills small group or classroom guidance sessions. Publicize important dates and registration details for college entrance tests. Outreach as appropriate for tenth, eleventh, and twelfth grade students.
- Make plans for National School Counselor Week.

February

- Celebrate National School Counselor Week.
- Continue transition planning for all students.
- Plan grade level college and career readiness events, including FAFSA information sessions or completion events.
- Continue classroom and small group counseling program related to career awareness and skills.

- Continue individual planning meetings with all students. Take notes for future letters of recommendation. Include awards, extracurricular activities, volunteer work, and special strengths.
- Review students' individual learning plans. Revise and further develop as necessary.
- Hold test information and interpretation sessions for students and families.
- Continue test-taking skills small group or classroom guidance sessions. Publicize important dates and registration details for college entrance tests. Outreach as appropriate for tenth, eleventh, and twelfth grade students.
- Attend or organize college and career fairs, activities, or special sessions.

March

- Continue classroom and small group counseling program related to career awareness and skills.
- Implement grade level college and career readiness events.
- Continue individual planning meetings with all students. Take notes for future letters of recommendation. Include awards, extracurricular activities, volunteer work, and special strengths.
- Continue transition planning for all students.
- Attend or organize college and career fairs, activities, or special sessions.
- Review students' individual learning plans. Revise and further develop as necessary.
- Plan grade level college and career readiness events, including FAFSA information sessions or completion events.
- Continue test-taking skills small group or classroom guidance sessions. Publicize important dates and registration details for college entrance tests. Outreach as appropriate for tenth, eleventh, and twelfth grade students.

April

- Continue classroom and small group counseling program related to career awareness and skills.
- Attend or organize college and career fairs, activities, or special sessions.
- Review students' individual learning plans. Revise and further develop as necessary.
- Continue transition planning.

May

- Conclude classroom and small group counseling program related to career awareness and skills for the year.
- Continue transition planning.

June

- Evaluate current college and career readiness program.
- Review and share data and outcomes with all stakeholders.
- Set college and career readiness goals for following academic year.

References

Allen, W. (2005). A forward glance in a mirror: Diversity challenged–access, equity, and success in higher education. *Educational Researcher, 34*(7), 18–23.

American School Counselor Association. (2014). *Mindsets and behaviors for student success: K–12 college- and career-readiness standards for every student.* Alexandria, VA: Author.

American School Counselor Association. (2016). The school counselor and school-family-community partnerships. Alexandria, VA: Author.

American Psychiatric Association. (2013). Specific learning disorder fact sheet. Arlington, VA: American Psychiatric Publishing. Retrieved April 8, 2016, from http://www.dsm5.org.

Arnold, K. D., Lu, E. C., & Armstrong, K. J. (2012). Special issue: The ecology of college readiness. *ASHE Higher Education Report, 38*(5), 1–138.

Auger, R. W., Blackhurst, A. E., & Wahl, K. H. (2005). The development of elementary-aged children's career aspirations and expectations. *Professional School Counseling, 8*(4), 322–329.

Austin, A., & Oseguera, L. (2004). The declining equity of American higher education. *Review of Higher Education, 27*(3), 321–341.

Barnhardt, C., Ramos, M., & Reyes, K. (2013). Equity and inclusion in practice: Administrative responsibility for fostering undocumented Students' learning. *About Campus, 18*(2), 20–26.

Berg, G. A. (2010). *Low-income students and the perpetuation of inequality: Higher education in America.* Farnham, Surrey, England: Ashgate.

Blackwell, E., & Pinder, P. J. (2014). What are the motivational factors of first generation minority college students who overcome their family histories to pursue higher education? *College Student Journal, 48*(1), 45–56.

Bryan, J., & Holcomb-McCoy, C. (2004). School counselors' perceptions of their involvement in school-family-community partnerships. *Professional School Counseling, 8,* 219–227.

Bryan, J., Moore-Thomas, C., Day-Vines, N., & Holcomb-McCoy, C. (2011). School counselors as social capital: The effects of high school college counseling on college application rates. *Journal of Counseling and Development, 89,* 190–199.

Chen, X. (2005). *First generation students in postsecondary education: A look at their college transcripts* (NCES 2005–171). U.S. Department of Education, National Center for Education Statistics. Washington, DC: U.S. Government Printing Office.

Cianciotto, J., & Cahill, S. (2003). *Education policy: Issues affecting lesbian, gay, bisexual, and transgender youth.* New York: The National Gay and Lesbian Task Force Policy Institute.

Cortiella, C., & Horowitz, S. H. (2014). *The state of learning disabilities: Facts, trends and emerging issues.* New York: National Center for Learning Disabilities.

Council for the Accreditation of Counseling and Related Educational Programs (CACREP). (2016). 2016 CACREP standards. Retrieved from http://www.cacrep.org/for-programs/2016-cacrep-standards/.

Croninger, R. G., & Lee, V. E. (2001). Social capital and dropping out of high school: Benefits to at-risk students of teachers' support and guidance. *Teachers College Record, 103,* 548–581.

Epstein, J. L., & Sanders, M. G. (2006). Prospects for change: Preparing educators for school, family, and community partnerships. *Peabody Journal of Education, 81,* 81–120.

Epstein, J. L., Sanders, M. G., Sheldon, S. B., Simon, B., Salinas, K., et al. (2002). *School, family, and community partnerships: Your handbook for action* (2nd ed.). Thousand Oaks, CA: Corwin Press.

Epstein, J. L., & Sheldon, S. B. (2016). Necessary but not sufficient: The role of policy for advancing programs of school, family, and community partnerships. *RSF: The Russell Sage Foundation Journal of The Social Sciences, 2*(5), 202–219.

Epstein, J. L., & Van Voorhis, F. L. (2010). School counselors' roles in developing partnerships with families for student success. *Professional School Counseling, 14,* 1–14.

Ferguson, R. F. (1999). Conclusion: Social science research, urban problems and community development alliances. In R. F. Ferguson & W. T. Dickens (Eds.), *Urban Problems and Community Development* (pp. 569–610). Washington, DC: Brookings Institution Press.

Gottfredson, L. S. (1981). Circumscription and compromise: A developmental theory of occupational aspirations. *Journal of Counseling Psychology, 28,* 545–579.

Gottfredson, G. D., & Johnstun, M. L. (2009). John Holland's contributions: A theory-ridden approach to career assistance. *Career Development Quarterly, 58*(2), 99–107.

Havlik, S., Schultheis, K., Schneider, K., & Neason, E. (2016). Local liaisons: Roles, challenges, and training in serving children and youth experiencing homelessness. *Urban Education,* 31. doi:10.1177/0042085916668954.

Henderson, A. T., & Mapp, K. L. (Eds.). (2002). *A new wave of evidence: The impact of school, family, community connections on student achievement.* Austin, TX: National Center for Family and Community Connections with Schools, South-west Educational Development Laboratory. Retrieved from https://www.sedl.org/connections/resources/evidence.pdf.

Hernandez. D. J., & Napierala, J. S. (2012). Children in immigrant families: Essential to America's future. An FCD Child and Youth Well-Being Index (CWI) Policy Brief. Foundation for Child Development. Retrieved April 21, 2015, from https://www.fcd-us.org/children-in-immigrant-families-essential-to-americas-future/.

Holcomb-McCoy, C. (2010). Involving low-income parents and parents of color in college readiness activities: An exploratory study. *Professional School Counseling*, *14*, 115–124.

Holland, J. L. (1970). *The self-directed search for career planning*. Palo Alto, CA: Consulting Psychologists Press.

Holland, J. L. (1997). *Making vocational choices: A theory of vocational personalities and work environments* (3rd ed.). Odessa, FL: Psychological Assessment Resources.

Horsford, S., & Sampson, C. (2013). High ELL growth states: Experiencing funding equity and opportunity for English language learners. *VUE: Voices in Urban Education, 37,* 47–54.

Hussar, W. J., & Bailey, T. M. (2017). *Projections of education statistics to 2025* (NCES 2017–019). U.S. Department of Education, Washington, DC: National Center for Education Statistics. Retrieved June 9, 2018, from https://nces.ed.gov/pubs2017/2017019.pdf.

Kosciw, J. G., Greytak, E. A., Palmer, N. A., & Boesen, M. J. (2014). *The 2013 National School Climate Survey: The experiences of lesbian, gay, bisexual and transgender youth in our nation's schools*. New York: GLSEN.

Lent, R. W., Brown, S. D., & Hackett, G. (2000). Contextual supports and barriers to career choice: A social cognitive analysis. *Journal of Counseling Psychology, 47,* 36–49.

Lightweis, S. (2014). The challenges, persistence, and success of white, working-class, first generation college students. *College Student Journal*, *48*(3), 461–467.

Morgan, B., deBruin, G., & Bruin, K. (2015). Constructing Holland's hexagon in South Africa: Development and initial validation of the South African career interest inventory. *Journal of Career Assessment, 23,* 493–511.

National Career Development Association (NCDA). (2009). Multicultural career counseling minimum competencies. Retrieved from https://www.ncda.org/aws/NCDA/pt/sp/guidelines.

National Career Development Association (NCDA). (2015). 2015 NCDA code of ethics. Retrieved from https://www.ncda.org/aws/NCDA/asset_manager/get_file/3395/ncda_code_of_ethics_for_web.pdf.

National Center for Education Statistics (NCES). (2015). PISA 2015 results. Retrieved from https://nces.ed.gov/surveys/pisa/pisa2015/index.asp.

National Center on Family Homelessness. (2014). *America's youngest outcast: A report card on child homelessness*. Retrieved from http://www.homelesschildrenamerica.org/mediadocs/280.pdf.

Nguyen, D. H. K., & Serna, G. R. (2014). Access or barrier? Tuition and fee legislation for undocumented students across the states. *Clearing House: A Journal of Educational Strategies, Issues and Ideas, 87*(3), 124–129.

Niles, S., & Harris-Bowlsbey, J. (2013). *Career development interventions in the 21st century* (4th ed.). Upper Saddle River, NJ: Pearson.

Osborn, D. S. (2002). *Using the self-directed search career explorer with middle school students: The practicality of Holland's RIASEC theory.* Retrieved from ERIC database. (ED465915).

Payne, E., & Smith, M. (2012). Rethinking safe schools approaches for LGBTQ students: Changing the questions we ask. *Journal of Perspectives in Multicultural Education, 14*, 187–193.

Perez, W. (2010). Higher education access for undocumented students: Recommendations for counseling professionals. *Journal of College Admission* (206), 32–35.

Reardon, R. C., & Lumsden, J. A. (2002). *Holland-based career materials: A resource list for educators.* Retrieved from ERIC database. (ED465917).

Rendon, L. (1998). Access in a democracy: Narrowing the opportunity gap. In *Reconceptualizing Access in Post Secondary Education: Report of the Policy Panel on Access* (pp. 57–70). Washington, DC: National Center for Education Statistics.

Rounds, J. B., & Tracey, T. J. (1996). Cross-cultural structural equivalence of RIASEC models and measures. *Journal of Counseling Psychology, 43*, 310–329.

Sanlo, R., & Espinoza, L. (2012). Risk and retention: Are LGBTQ students staying in your community college? *Community College Journal of Research and Practice, 36*(7), 475–481.

Savickas, M. (2012). Life design: A paradigm for career intervention in the 21st century. *Journal of Counseling and Development, 90*, 13–19.

Solberg, V. S., Wills, J., Redmon, K., & Skaff, L. (2014). *Use of individualized learning plans as a promising practice for driving college and career readiness efforts: Findings and recommendations from a multi-method, multi-study effort.* Washington, DC: National Collaborative on Workforce and Disability for Youth, Institute for Educational Leadership.

Super, D. E. (1980). A life-span, life-space approach to career development. *Journal of Vocational Behavior, 13*, 282–298.

Tang, M. (2009). Examining the application of Holland's theory to vocational interests and choices of Chinese college students. *Journal of Career Assessment, 17*(1), 86–98.

Torey, E. (2015, March). Clusters, pathways, and BLS: Connecting career information. Career Outlook, U.S. Bureau of Labor Statistics. Retrieved August 17, 2017, from https://www.bls.gov/careeroutlook/2015/article/career-clusters.htm#.

U.S. Department of Education. (2012, July 14). *Overview of the financial aid process.* Retrieved May 8, 2018, from https://www.youtube.com/watch?v=kbJ55UWMEFE.

U.S. Department of Education. (2012, August 20). *Types of federal student aid.* Retrieved May 8, 2018, from https://www.youtube.com/watch?annotation_id=annotation_2419155109&feature=iv&list=PL5164CE4355C66FCB&src_vid=H_iS7gmQd9o&v=Pn4OECMTh5w.

U.S. Department of Education, National Center for Education Statistics. (2011). *Comparative indicators of education in the United States and other G-8 countries 2011: Reading achievement by immigrant status.* Retrieved April 21, 2015, from http://nces.ed.gov/pubs2012/2012007/section2f.asp.

U.S. Department of Education, National Center for Education Statistics. (2013). *Digest of Education Statistics, 2012* (NCES 2014–015), chapter 3.

U.S. Department of Education, National Center for Education Statistics. (2014). *The condition of education 2014* (NCES 2014–083), English Language Learners.

U.S. Department of Education, National Center for Education Statistics. (2015). *Digest of Education Statistics, 2013* (NCES 2015–011), Table 204.30.

Wang, F. K. (2014, September 2). *As students of color surpass Whites, A closer look at numbers*. NBC News. Retrieved March 16, 2014, from http://www.nbcnews.com/news/asian-america/students-color-surpass-whites-closer-look-numbers-n193811.

Index

access, 7–9
advocacy, 18
American School Counselor Association, 24, 35, 42
ASCA. *See* American School Counselor Association
attention deficit disorder (ADD), 12–13
attention deficit/hyperactivity disorder (ADHD), 12–13

bias, 19, 37–38

career cluster, 53, 82, 106–107
career counseling, 8, 23–25, 30, 32, 96–97
career development: awareness, 33, 50–54, 58–61, 78–82, 106–107; readiness, 5, 69–71; planning, 33, 96–99
college: awareness, 55–57, 82–83, 101–103; first generation students, 9–10
community development alliance, 39–40
constructivist approach, 30
counseling relationship, 17–18
cultural competence, 8–9, 18, 20, 25, 30–31, 45, 64, 114–115

decision making, 96–97
deficit thinking, 37
developmental approach, 3–5

educator's paradigm, 45–46
English language learner (ELL), 15
entrepreneurship, 74–76
Epstein, J. L., 41
equity, 7–9
ethics, 24–25
evaluation, 117–118

Ferguson, R. F., 39–40
financial aid, 99–101

gen alpha, 3
generation z, 3
goal setting, 22, 69–74,
Gottfredson, L. S., 30–32, 47, 66, 91; circumscription and compromise, 30–32

Holland, J. L., 25–28
homelessness, 11

immigrants, 14–16
individual learning plan (ILP), 21, 63–64

job skills, 95–96, 98–99

learning disabilities, 12
lifespan/life space theory, 28–29
LGBTQ, 14,19
low income, 10

McKinney-Vento Act, 11–12

narrative approach, 30
National Career Development Association (NCADA), 24
needs assessment, 45, 91–93
non-cognitive skills, 57–58, 85, 108–109

partnership characteristics, 36–37
Plyler vs. Doe, 16
poverty, 10–12
Program for International Student Assessment (PISA), 8

Savickas, M.: life design intervention model, 30
self-awareness, 72–73
social capital, 16–17, 43
social cognitive career theory, 32, 90
social skills, 57–58, 85, 108–109
Solberg, V. S., 63
strength-based approaches, 38, 42
stress management, 103–105
students of color, 13
study skills, 48–49, 77–78
Super, D. E., 28–29, 47, 65, 90

technology, 61, 85, 110, 115–117
time management, 55–56, 67–68
transition planning, 21, 105–106

undocumented students, 15–16

About the Author

Cheryl Moore-Thomas received her PhD in counselor education from the University of Maryland. She is professor of education and the associate vice president of faculty affairs and diversity at Loyola University Maryland. Moore-Thomas has served as the associate dean of the School of Education; school counseling program director; co-director, administrator, and director of Loyola's College Advising Corps; and in several public school system positions. Over her professional career, she has published and presented in the areas of multicultural counseling competence in school counseling, cultural identity development of children and adolescents, college access counseling, and accountability in school counseling programs.

www.ingramcontent.com/pod-product-compliance
Lightning Source LLC
Chambersburg PA
CBHW030142240426
43672CB00005B/231